Fear, Fun & Faith

The remarkable story of a Diversity Award winner

John Flanner

Revised Edition, Published by John Flanner in 2009, 2015

Printed by Biddles in 2015

Biddles
Castle House,
E Winch Rd,
Blackborough End,
King's Lynn,
Norfolk
PE32 1SF

A catalogue record for this book is available from the British Library.

ISBN 978-0-9934175-0-4

Typeset in Calibri 11pt by Rachel Edwards Writes.
Cover design by Studio D.
Printed in Great Britain

Contents

Foreword

As the one time US President Franklin D. Roosevelt once said, "The only things we have to fear is fear itself". Sometimes the fear of something can be more destructive than the thing in question.

With my background of a career in Law, I have sadly encountered many people experiencing fear. Some of it justified, some not. But if we are honest, there is not one of us over a certain age who can say that fear has never impinged upon our lives at some stage. Many adults are acutely aware of the phobias and hang ups which they carry daily with them, often these fears are personal, trivial and have no legal implications – they are not rooted in dramatic injustices, but perhaps are simply grounded in long term aversions, which have sadly developed over time.

This book is not a self-help guide and does not pretend to be. Instead it is a frank revelation from someone who began to struggle with a host of fears from within, before being afflicted with unexpected disability from without. What followed was plenty of tears and no little dearth of embarrassing moment before the process of overcoming such fears eventually proved triumphant.

What became of John's experience may not be replicated identically in the experience of others. The path for life which he proposes will be greeted sceptically by some, but many of us have known what it is like to wake up in the morning and immediately dread the day ahead, whether it will be one spent at home, work or in education. Some reading this are people who feel apprehension and inadequacy at the thought of certain social situations and activities. This book does not claim to have all the answers, but it shows that (deeply entrenched) feelings are not uncommon and that there is hope, and that it doesn't always have to be this way.

Diversity is a modern buzzword and through these pages you will get a flavour of Midlands life, a reminder how things were growing up in Birmingham in the 1960's and 1970's – a time of industrial and racial strife, dimpled beer mugs and Love Thy Neighbour on ITV. You will also get a hint, at best, of what it must be like to live with near total blindness. During his story, John even attempts to take an honest look at perhaps the root of all fear; fear of death.

John and I go back a long way, and like me, he is a Brummie with Solihull connections. We used to go to the same church years ago, we love music and support Aston Villa; both Villains!

I fully endorse John Flanner on a personal and professional level. I hope you enjoy his story, but more importantly gain from it.

Rt. Hon. Lord Taylor of Warwick

House of Lords
Palace of Westminster
London

Dedication

'Rose Of My Heart'

We're the best partners this world's ever seen
Together as close as can be
But sometimes it's hard to find time in between
To tell you what you are to me

You are the rose of my heart
You are the love of my life
A flower not faded or falling apart
If you're tired, rest your head on my arm
Rose of my heart.

When sorrow holds you in her arms of clay
It's raindrops that fall from your eyes
Your smile is the dun come to earth for the day
You brighten my blackest of skies

You are the rose of my heart
You are the love of my life
A flower not faded or falling apart
If you're cool, let my love make your warm
Rose of my heart.

So hard times are easy times, what do I care?
There's nothing I'd change if I could
The tears and the laughter are things that we share
Your hand in mine makes all times good

You are the rose of my heart
You are the love of my life
A flower not faded or falling apart
You're my harbour in life's restless storm
Rose of my heart.

(Performed by Johnny Cash, words and music by Hugh Moffatt).

Introduction

Easter Monday 25th March 2005

As I sit at my computer today I realise that this is something of a crossroads for me. I am coming up to 58 years of age and in theory I can retire in just over two years' time. However, from a financial and conviction point of view I need to continue working. It is true to say that from a career perspective I am more interested in refirement than retirement. I cannot escape the thought that I was put on this planet for a purpose and with a specific destiny to fulfil.

My life has been interesting, varied and challenging to date but there is no sense whatsoever in my heart that it is now a case of 'mission accomplished'. On the contrary, I feel that the best of me (and for me) is yet to come. In the course of living your life you will no doubt come across people who are multi-talented. They seem to be experts at such a wide variety of different things. I have often felt intimidated by such people and at times wondered where I was when God was dishing out the talents. I class myself as a one or two talent person and it has taken me most of my life to begin to appreciate what those talents are.

I am told that I have the ability to encourage and inspire people of all ages thanks to the gift that I have been given of being able to communicate both orally and in writing. I will explain later in the book how these talents/gifts were released to me. For the moment, however, it has been confirmed to me just how powerful these gifts are thanks to a project I have undertaken as part of my job at the Inland Revenue over the past couple of years.

It all began when I wrote a disability-related article for our office magazine, and to my surprise one of our Area Directors, John Dolan, picked up the phone to say thank you for the article and to congratulate me on the way it had been written. He was also enlightened by its contents, which highlighted a disability email forum that had been set up nationally across the then Inland Revenue, now Her Majesty's Revenue and Customs (HMRC).

The same Director then followed up this by recommending that I enrol on a personal development programme, which the Department were hosting in Coventry. Typical of me, feeling somewhat insecure about this, I said I felt it would be great if I was 25 years of age, but as I was 56 maybe it was a little too late for me. Thankfully he would have none of that, saying that I had an obvious gift in the field of communication and he would like to see that being developed. I can honestly say that I have rarely come across anyone who was so positively on my side and wanting me to succeed as much as John did at that time. So it was that I applied to go on the programme and was accepted.

The programme was called 'Breakthrough' and it covered such topics as Making Positive Personal Affirmations, Dreams and Visions, The Power of Forgiveness and Developing Goal Setting Skills. Those early seminars were so dynamic and left me thinking "I wish I had been taught these things at school – they would have changed the course of my life". The ethos behind Breakthrough can be summed up in the following affirmations which we were encouraged to speak out and begin each day with:

"My future is in **my** own hands, change **is** possible, and **I** have the ability to make the necessary changes."

Why not write down those three statements and begin to speak them into your life on a daily basis? You might just find that something amazing starts to happen! As a result of what I learned on the Breakthrough programme I now believe I could have achieved my desire to become a sports journalist. However at the tender age of 15, when I was informed by the Careers Officer that I had to gain five GCE 'O' Level passes I gave up on my dream, thinking I was not intelligent enough for that. My mind was telling me lies. A little bit of encouragement at that stage may well have worked wonders.

Breakthrough also taught me that every person has a genius inside of them just waiting to be released in some way. I go along with the Biblical view that says we are all created in the image of God, who is himself a genius, and has put part of his genius inside each of his superb creations. I now realise that many children have their dreams stolen by well meaning, but cynical adults who in turn had their childhood dreams stolen by cynical adults. It's a cycle that keeps on being repeated. Some kids are strong-minded enough to press on with their dreams regardless, but many have their dreams crushed and live their whole lives with a feeling of what might have been if only... "Dear God, please don't let me become a stealer of dreams but allow me to encourage and help people of all ages realise their potential".

Two other ingredients of Breakthrough, were a mentoring relationship and to undertake a project that would benefit the business overall. My mentor Ruth, an Area Director from Merry Hill in the West Midlands, was very good for me because she held me accountable for suggestions and ideas that I came up with. I have never been short of ideas but have often lacked the confidence or discipline to put them into action. As far as a project was concerned, Ruth came up with the idea that I should put together a talk under the umbrella of Diversity Awareness. I protested mildly that I did not know anything about Diversity, but she insisted that I was diverse. I think that was the word she used and not perverse! Ruth said that I had dispelled a lot of the preconceptions she had about blind people and in terms of my attitude to life I certainly brought a different approach compared to many other people.

I gave the matter some thought, and once I had put down in writing what I wanted to say, I then had to actively seek out opportunities to go and talk at team meetings around the building. I had worked for the Inland Revenue for 22 years as an audio typist, never doing anything else. However, if I was going to develop some of this talent for communicating, I had to make a start somewhere.

In City Centre House, where I work, in the centre of Birmingham, there are approximately 800 members of staff, so plenty of teams to approach. I sent an email to all managers requesting an opportunity to attend team meetings to give a short presentation on the subject of Diversity Awareness. I gave the matter further thought and very soon the invitations started rolling in. My first talk to our Business Support Team was for a 15 minute duration, and thinking that the title of Diversity Awareness sounded a bit dry, I subtitled it 'Fear, Fun and Faith'.

The meeting went really well and at one point several people were wiping tears from their eyes whilst a moment or two later they were laughing heartily at some of my stories. At the end of the talk there was a steady stream of questions, followed later by a flow of congratulatory and appreciative emails.

After that initial meeting others followed and slowly but surely my time was increased to the point where I am now being invited to speak for one hour at meetings. The response from people has been truly amazing and I have since taken this talk across the country to HMRC staff in places such as Peterborough, Ipswich, Norwich, Leeds, Leicester Coventry, Lincoln and Milton Keynes, speaking to some of the senior management within HMRC.

Even since starting to write this book I have been honoured by the Department with an invitation to attend a champagne dinner at the London Park Lane Hilton to celebrate with others the work that has been done in raising awareness of Diversity and Equal Opportunities. The feedback from staff has said that my talk is not only humorous, but also inspiring and highly motivational. Numerous people have said that I should write a book so that others can benefit from my experiences and insights.

What follows is an expanded version of the Fear, Fun and Faith talks that have taken HMRC by storm and me by surprise. I sincerely hope you enjoy it, have a few laughs along the way and feel inspired to grab your life by the scruff of the neck, so that you begin to walk more purposefully into your God appointed destiny.

John Flanner, Solihull, West Midlands

Blind beginnings

"I'm sorry Mr Flanner there's nothing more we can do. John will have to be registered blind".

The Eye Consultant, Mr Vernon-Smith at Birmingham Eye Hospital was talking to my Dad after I had been attending the outpatient's clinic for around six months. I was employed at Fort Dunlop, part of the Dunlop Rubber Co in Birmingham, as a sales clerk in the Motor Cycle Tyre Sales Department. One morning I was checking a balance sheet and found it difficult to read some of the figures. I took the balance sheet back to the typist and said, "I am sorry Pam, but this will need to be retyped because some of the figures are blurred."

Pam, looked up and took the balance sheet from me and then rather quizzically said, "But John, this is perfectly clear".

She gave it me back and I looked again saying, "No it isn't, look at these" and in that moment my mind went back to a Sunday football game I had played a week or two earlier when I had experienced blurred vision during a rainstorm and also to another occasion when I had sustained a slight bang on the head during a game, again leaving me with temporary blurring in the left eye. Now I knew something was seriously wrong.

"Don't worry Pam, I'll sort it", I said in a worried tone.

I went straight to my boss, explained the situation and he gave me permission to go and see the firm's optician. I did, and on examination I was referred to the Birmingham Eye Hospital immediately. By now, my eyes were the talk of the office and when I returned to explain that I had been referred to the hospital there were a few worried faces around. Despite offers to accompany me to the hospital in Birmingham city centre, I decided to go alone catching the number 66 bus not far from the office. Tests on that first hospital visit confirmed a significant loss of sight in the left eye, though at that stage the right eye was perfect. After about 45 minutes and several tests I was told that I could go home but I would need to return at the same time the following week and that was the pattern for the next six months up until now.

In that time my sight had deteriorated week after week to the point where both eyes were now affected and for my own safety and that of others, I needed to be escorted. I could not even do my job anymore and so was on long term sick. Funnily enough, having got over the initial shock, I was quite enjoying my afternoons at the hospital and any time now I thought they would give me some tablets, put in some drops or perform a minor operation and then I would be okay. So now, therefore, to hear these words being spoken to my Dad in response to his question, "When are you going to do something?" was, as it were, a bolt from the blue.

"What do you mean, there's nothing you can do?" Dad asked.

"John is suffering from a very rare hereditary condition called Leber's Optic Atrophy and there is no cure" said Mr Vernon-Smith.

My mind went back to a film I had watched only a couple of days before. Reach for the Sky starring Kenneth More as Douglas Bader, the World War II hero who had to have both of his legs amputated. One particular scene of the film stayed with me. Douglas is lying in his hospital bed in a state of semi-consciousness when he overhears two nurses talking at the foot of his bed.

"How is he doing?" asked one nurse.

"Not good, I think he's given up" said the other.

Apparently it was at that point when Douglas Bader said to himself, "I'll show them" and that is the attitude which rose up inside of me as I listened into this conversation between the Consultant and my Dad on that spring morning in 1967. Having completed the necessary forms we left the hospital in something of a daze. Mum was waiting anxiously at home, but Dad and I delayed the inevitable by going for a coffee at the Kardoma coffee shop in Colmore Row. The shop was not very busy and Dad left me at a window seat while he went up to the counter. There was a radio playing in the shop and the news headlines came on. I was shocked and saddened by what I heard.

"Donald Campbell has been killed in a crash on Lake Coniston while attempting to break the world water speed record," said the BBC newsreader.

"Here's your coffee, son" said Dad, as tears streamed down my face.

Dad reached out, touched my hand and said, "I'm sorry son".

"That's okay Dad", I said, "but what about Donald Campbell, that is terrible..."

The fact was that at that moment I was far more upset about the death of Donald Campbell than I was about the fact that I had just been registered blind.

Dad and I eventually arrived home to our ground floor maisonette on the Wyrley Birch Council Estate in Erdington, Birmingham. Mum was devastated at the news of course, especially as the diagnosis was that the condition had come from her side of the family. Mum and Dad were to have two further crushing blows later because my sister Joan and brother Paul were later to go blind also.

I don't think Mum ever fully got over these emotional hammer blows and like many, I live with the regret that I did not give my dear mother anywhere near enough love, respect and understanding she deserved while she was alive. She was the kind of Mum who waited on us hand and foot and I took her so much for granted. I take great comfort in the fact however that before she died of cancer on 23 August 1986, she had some 10 weeks beforehand put her trust in Jesus Christ as her Lord and Saviour, so to that end I am confident that I will see her again one day to let her know that I love her, am not sorry for this condition and that I am grateful for the life she gave me.

I am the eldest of four children. My parents Francis (Frank) and Marjorie were married in St Paul's Church in the Lozells area of Birmingham on 20 April 1946 and I arrived at Heathfield Road Maternity Hospital, Handsworth on 29 July 1947. Almost two years later my sister Joan was born. When I was 4 years of age my parents moved from their house in Aston to a back-to-back council house in Scott Street, Vauxhall.

Our house had an attic, which was my bedroom and across the road was the London Midland Scottish (LMS) main railway line and when the high-speed steam trains went through to Vauxhall and Duddeston station the bedroom windows would rattle. It was a great room for train spotting so I quickly developed that hobby. When I heard the sound of a train coming along the track I would dive out of bed, train-spotting book in hand and peer out of the window. I would make a note of the train number or name and then find it in my book and underline it very neatly in red ink.

It was not too long after moving to that house that my brother Paul was born and then my sister Susan followed a little while after that. We had great fun growing up in that neighbourhood, despite the fact that we did not have a lot of the luxuries we enjoy today. The lavatory was situated in the back yard which we shared with our neighbours at the rear, bath time was once a week and consisted of a tin bath in front of the living room coal fire. Mum had to pour in several saucepans full of hot water before it was deep enough to get into. We also had a 9 inch black and white television with just one BBC channel to look at. I do remember ITV starting however and the first programme we watched was *Sunday Night at the London Palladium*.

As kids we played lots of street games with many other children. The girls would be out playing with their dolls and prams, skipping ropes while the boys, if not playing cowboys and Indians, would often be playing football in the middle of the concrete road or cricket against the lampposts, which we used for the wickets. It was in that environment that I developed my love for football. The games in the street would go on for hours at times and occasionally we would carry the game over to the next day or two if necessary. The tackles would fly in hard and fast and there were many cut knees to prove it – I have the scars on each knee to this day.

I attended Loxton Street Infant and Junior School where I was very happy, apart from a few glaring exceptions. The first of these was my very first day at the age of 5. I will never forget that smell as long as I live. I don't know whether it was the polish on the desks, the bleach on the floors or a horrendous cocktail of a few things. It was horrible and I came to identify it as the 'school' smell. Somehow it was austere and scary and I cried to go home. However I had to stay and eventually, as you do, I got used to it to the point that I did not notice that smell any more, until I came across it unexpectedly that is.

Another bad experience both took place in school assembly, which incidentally I used to very much enjoy. It was the singing of the hymns that I found inspiring even though I had no idea what most of the words meant. One morning I was singing heartily away, probably Onward Christian Soldiers, a particular favourite of the school, when suddenly one of the bigger boys in front elbowed me in the stomach and said, "Shut your foghorn Flanner".

I was stunned, not to mention winded, and as it turned out, deeply hurt. I say that because from then on, even though I still loved the songs, I only ever mimed the words. More drastic than that I have been very self-conscious about my voice ever since. I have since learned that God loves it when we make a joyful noise, so at least as far as he is concerned I am okay. Another powerful illustration of the power that words can have over us for good or bad, for positive or negative. I trust that, like me, you no longer believe the old rhyme that says, "Sticks and stones may break my bones but names will never hurt me".

18

One of my most vivid and wonderful memories of school took place when I was just turned 11 years of age. By this time I was attending Hastings Road Secondary Modern Boys, Perry Common, after my parents had moved house to a first floor modern maisonette. It was luxury by comparison to Scott Street and we overlooked a lovely park by the name of Witton Lakes. I desperately wanted to be in the school football team but until then had never made it as a regular.

On this particular Friday lunchtime I was walking along the corridor when I stopped to check out the notice board. On that board were printed the names of all the people who would be in the various school teams the following day. I stared and could hardly believe my eyes. My name was there, number 10 J Flanner. As I looked I could feel my chest swell with pride and excitement. I ran all the way home to tell Mum. "I'm in the team Mum" I shouted, and there I stayed right up until I left school at the age of 15.

To be chosen in that way to join the team gave me so much confidence and for a few years I cherished a desire to become a professional footballer one day. That is what happens when someone chooses and approves of you, you actually do believe that you are good and that you have a worthwhile contribution to make. Once realising that I was not quite good enough to make it professionally, I then conceived the ill-fated dream of becoming a writer – or maybe it was not so ill fated after all!

At this point I want to place on record my love and passion for Aston Villa Football Club. This is an affair that was fanned into flame at a very young age when I attended games with my Dad. I first attended our magnificent home ground of Villa Park in 1956 to watch the Villa reserves play and fell in love with the place immediately. It is a ground of incredible history, character and charm. For me there has always been something magical about the atmosphere of the place. Aston Villa Football Club was born out of a young men's Bible Class in the mid-19th Century and was part of Aston Villa Wesleyan Chapel. In fact it was our first Chairman, a Scotsman by the name of William McGregor who was the main inspiration behind the formation of the Football League and its inaugural twelve clubs.

Apart from the ground itself, there have been many great characters who have worn the claret and blue shirt with pride regardless of their ability. I have so many wonderful memories as a Villa fan and I intend to encapsulate these in a separate book, but one of the most enduring and emotional ones was in the last Cup final at the old Wembley Stadium before it was demolished.

The game was between Aston Villa and Chelsea and even though we lost a very poor game 1-0 I will always remember singing (not miming) the FA Cup Final hymn *Abide with Me*, turning to my son Ian and giving him a hug. We both had tears in our eyes as only a few years before, Ian had almost died when he went down with encephalitis (a virus on the brain) and was within a whisker of death.

On that May afternoon in London as over 70,000 people sang *Abide With Me*, I got to the line *"In life in death, oh Lord, abide with me"* and I said thank you to God for sparing the life of my dear son.

By then, my own life journey had not been without its fair share of heartache and emotion. Join me now as I endeavour to take you on a journey through what it feels like to be blind.

Section One – FEAR

Fear is an emotion which every person will experience at some time in their life. Sadly, however, for some people fear is something that grips them on a daily basis and many lives are paralysed by fear. Some fears are quite understandable of course, whilst others are totally illogical and phobic in their manifestation.

I have often been asked, especially by schoolchildren, who enquire with great enthusiasm and excitement in the voices, "John, what does it feel like to be blind?" With those kids I often feel like adding the word "wow" at the end of their question because they sound rather envious and would love to try being blind for a while. In some cases I have actually blindfolded the children and allowed them to walk around with my white stick so that they can get a feel of what it is like and they usually love it.

I have said that fear was a major emotion and in those early days as a registered blind person the fears came thick and fast. If you have never experienced problems with your sight, it is understandable that you wouldn't realise the challenges and fears you are faced with, so firstly let me list them before explaining how they were overcome;

- Fear of never going out alone again in case of accident.
- Fear of having to hold onto someone else's arm (particularly if it was a man). What would people think?
- Fear of eating in public.
- Fear of what would be going in my mouth when eating.
- Fear of never working again.
- Fear of being single.

Fear of failure

The fear of failure was something I was aware of from a young age, though of course I would not have put it in those terms. It manifested itself in me being ultra-cautious in whatever task I was given to do. At school for instance exam results were always published on the school notice board, starting with the number one right down to the bottom, a bit like the pop music charts. My big dread was seeing my name at the bottom of the list and so my heartfelt prayer was, "Please God don't let me finish bottom of the class." My thought was, "If only I could finish bottom but one, that would be great". I usually managed to finish up somewhere between sixth and tenth from the bottom and so I was enormously relieved when that happened.

In maths I would work slowly and methodically trying hard to get every answer right first time. Teachers often encouraged me to go faster but that might have meant making more mistakes. Years later after losing my sight, I went for an interview to be trained as a computer programmer. I had to sit a Braille test, containing 20 sequential mathematical questions. At the end of my one-hour exam I had completed six questions and to my delight I got all six right. Guess what, however, I did not pass and never did become a computer programmer. Those old fear-filled attitudes certainly do stick around don't they?

Fear of death

The fear of death is something that is common to many people and when I thought about it as a youngster it would send a cold shiver down my spine. This was not helped when a friend of mind told me after losing my sight, "My sister (she was a nurse) thinks you may have cancer of the eye". Now isn't that just what friends are for!!

I recall coming home from school one night when I was 10 years of age and seeing a headline on the newspaper stand, 'England Stars Killed in Plane Crash'. I soon discovered on arriving home that a plane carrying Manchester United players, staff and journalists had crashed on take-off from Munich Airport. I could hardly believe it or take it in. I had seen many of those players only a short while before in an exciting game at St Andrews. I had been standing by the halfway line, right at the front and the likes of legendary players Roger Byrne, David Pegg, Duncan Edwards and Tommy Taylor, who were almost within touching distance were now dead. It was almost impossible for me to take in.

In my teens I had some great mates and often on the way home from tenpin bowling, we would buy fish and chips and walk the two miles home late at night chatting away about issues of life and death. Often the stars would be shining brightly in the sky and we would discuss how they got there. Was it an accident or was there some genius called God who was behind it all. Those times of open discussion and debate were I believe really healthy for me; don't know about the fish and chips though!

Fear of the Dentist

As children in school we used to get regular visits from the dental nurse. Her visits were always greeted with a great deal of apprehension. As our names were called out we would join the queue and nervously wait to have our teeth examined. The lucky children would come back with nothing, but others would return carrying a form, which I recall had green print on it together with a stamp mark declaring either '20 minutes' or 'D'. Apparently the former meant a filling or two was needed, but the dreaded 'D' stood for decay and signalled a trip to the school dental clinic for an extraction.

Well after several successful visits to the nurse, my date with destiny came around and sure enough I received the dreaded 'D' stamp. Within a few weeks I was at the clinic accompanied by Mum and I honestly don't know who was more scared out of the two of us. I had to have several teeth removed.

Still shaking with fear, mainly from the smell of the place, I was sat back in a chair and a metal clamp-like device was put on my mouth so that it could be stretched uncomfortably wide open. A mask was then put on my face and the gas sent me to sleep. Even to this day the horrendous dream I had then is so vivid in my mind. I was taken high into the sky and then dropped and before I hit the ground I was lifted up again by a hook from my mouth and I could feel it pulling and ripping my mouth apart. Then I came back to consciousness, with blood everywhere and a gaping hole in my gums. It was a nightmare that I vowed even then never to repeat.

I was about 8 years of age then and I did not return to a dentist for many years. I know that many children of my generation can tell similar horror stories involving the school clinic. I am happy to say that many years later I had to face up to and overcome this fear. But I will come to that later in the 'Faith' section of this book.

Fear of swimming

As far as my fear of water goes, my earliest memory is of my sister Joan falling into an open-air swimming pool in Blackpool when we were very small children. As she fell in and screamed I ran for my Dad who jumped in and saved her. It was a pretty terrifying situation.

My real dislike of the water, however, came about when I found out that swimming was on the school timetable. We would all arrive at school on that day with our towels and swimwear, then at the appropriate time head off in an orderly fashion and march the half a mile or so to the public baths with teacher marching alongside to keep us in order. On entering the building that bleach smell got right up my nose, conjuring up a very negative emotion for me.

The boys and girls went off to their respective communal changing rooms. I felt incredibly embarrassed getting undressed in front of the other boys because I was so thin, compared to most of the others. It was a really tricky operation trying to get my trunks on without anyone seeing my private parts. Added to that it was freezing cold and I was shaking like a leaf in a gale.

As a non-swimmer I would look at the other boys and girls having such fun swimming up and down the pool and though it looked very appealing and indeed easy, I just could not pluck up the courage to let go of the rail and launch out. The cold water didn't help at all. I was shivering just as much if not more than in the changing room. The whole experience for me was an absolute nightmare and relief only came when we were marching back to school and I must confess that I felt much fresher for the experience of actually being in the water. However, that did not stop me from week after week begging Mum to write me a letter excusing me from swimming due to earache, cough or whatever else I could come up with.

I have come to realise over the years that God loves to set people free from all of their fears. One by one he has dealt with all of mine, but never in a pushy or pressurising way. Swimming to me looked so easy when I watched other people doing it and it looked so refreshing, especially on a hot day.

As I grew into adult life and had children of my own who themselves learned to swim, I found myself praying and asking God to help me overcome this fear. One day I was told that in Solihull where I was living a new club had been formed called 'Solihull Seals' and this was basically a group of people who were giving their time freely to take and teach disabled people to swim. I felt that God was on my case and providing an ideal opportunity for me.

I went along to the Tudor Grange swimming baths for several weeks on a Monday night and was introduced to a Dr McKenzie, then a local GP, I immediately felt confident with him in a way that I never did with the teachers at school. I trusted that he would not let me drown and within a few weeks he had me swimming and the 5 metres badge on my shorts for many years became one of my proudest possessions!

Fear of girls

This was undoubtedly the worst of all my fears. I don't really know how it came about, because as I said earlier I had two sisters with whom I got on well. Back in my infant and junior school days there was one girl I always liked the look of, and thought she was beautiful, but I don't think she ever spoke to me. As I grew older I still liked to look at girls, but I just lived to play football every moment of every day, but once in my teenage years I found myself becoming increasingly self-conscious.

Often, and especially before going out in the morning, I would stand in front of the mirror and tell myself how ugly I was. I had beady eyes, stick out ears, big nose, a big gap in the front of my teeth, scruffy hair that blew all over the place and besides all of that I was very skinny. The fact that I was in the 'A' stream at school, was a decent footballer, in the school PE team and had some good friends counted for nothing in my eyes. The girls' school was just a few hundred yards down the road from the boys' school so I would often see groups of girls standing together talking, laughing and invariably pointing in my direction. "No doubt mocking me", I thought to myself. This to me was a terrible handicap. There were times when I took a fancy to certain girls but I could never pluck up the courage to ask a girl for a date, because I was convinced she would reject me.

I have already mentioned that I worked at Dunlop in a tyre sales office. Part of my job was to take the invoices that were to be typed each morning to the typing pool. This was a huge pool of around 40 typists, all of them females of course. That was a really scary business for me, a bit like Daniel in the lions' den, except that I was no courageous Daniel. I tried hard to look relaxed and unperturbed as I walked briskly across the office not saying a word to anyone. I handed over the invoices to the supervisor and hurried hastily out again, convinced that there were a few derogatory comments made behind my back.

With these previous experiences, you can imagine my horror after going blind and having gone through a period of rehabilitation, to be then told that I would need to attend a college in London to be trained as an audio typist. This was after I had already been turned down for the computer programming training, even though I did get six out of six! The thought of spending my life as a typist and working with all of those women did not bear thinking about, but at least that was way off in the future.

Fear of going out

Newly registered as a blind person I arrived home from the hospital with Dad, still with the death of the great Donald Campbell uppermost in my mind. As was my custom I entered the maisonette, said hi to Mum and having discarded my coat over the handrail at the bottom of the stairs, headed off upstairs to the sanctuary of my bedroom. I shared the room with my brother Paul, who was then 13 years of age. Like many teenagers, I did not communicate a great deal with Mum and Dad at that time, but I took great consolation from my large collection of pop singles and albums. I had been buying records for about five years then, starting with *Things* by Bobby Darin, followed soon after by *The Swiss Maid* sung by Del Shannon. I proceeded to buy singles at a rate of about three per week, costing in total £1. I also got into buying albums (or LPs as they were called) though not as often as singles because of the price.

Apart from catchy tunes, I used to love listening to the lyrics of songs and often drew strength and encouragement from them. Oddly enough it was the sad songs that brought me most comfort, particularly those with a soul and Tamla Motown background. One glaring exception to this was the Beatles song called *Nowhere Man*. I loved the tune and the words:

Doesn't have a point of view/Knows not where he's going to/Isn't he a bit like you and me/Making all his nowhere plans for nobody

The song made me feel there's somebody else out there who feels like I do. So many songs made me feel happy inside and gave me strength. An album that was particularly enjoyable at this time was *I'll Take You Where The Music's Playing*, by the Drifters. I don't know what it was exactly, but that record had such an aura about it I felt that I was there at the party with them. Each track on the record was so full of atmosphere.

For around three months I spent hour after hour in my room playing music all day long and night times too. The noise must have driven my family and neighbours almost to the point of distraction, but I was too wrapped up in myself to realise that. The Searchers, Jim Reeves and Otis Reading were three of the acts that kept me company during these unnerving days of adjustment to my new and rapidly changing world.

My world of music and tears was interrupted rather abruptly one day when Mum knocked on my bedroom door and said, "There's a lady here to see you, she's from the Social Services".

I hurriedly followed Mum downstairs and on entering the living room I was greeted by the person who was to become a regular companion in my life for the next few months.

"Hello John, nice to meet you, my name is Miss Clews." (They were more formal in those days).

Mum and I sat down on the settee whilst Miss Clews began her discourse from the comfort of the armchair opposite.

"Well John", she said, "you've been registered for quite a few weeks now, so maybe it's time to draw up a plan to aid your rehabilitation. Have you given any thought as to what you might do in the future?"

"Not at all", I replied, "what is there to do?"

"Well there's quite a lot really", she answered in a warm, reassuring tone, "and that's why I am here, to look at our options."

I was aware of Mum sitting anxiously beside me puffing deeply on a cigarette wondering just what our young lady from Social Services was going to come up with. It transpired that I was first going to be offered some mobility training. That is learning to get around outside with the use of a white stick and then plans would be made for me to attend a rehabilitation centre in Torquay for three months. I recall taking a very deep breath at that point as fear raced through my senses. It was bad enough the thought of walking the streets of

Birmingham carrying a white stick let alone leaving home for three months; I had never been away from home in my life. I know that this came as a big blow to Mum also. I quickly realised however that both of these challenges had to be faced and overcome if I was ever going to do anything with my life.

Miss Clews began by visiting our home four mornings a week where I was given two hours each morning of mobility training. I was introduced to the symbol cane. This was a flimsy, plastic-coated aluminium stick that actually folded away into four smallish sections so that it could be put in a pocket if say, I went out to the pub. I remember thinking "that won't give me much protection", but least it wasn't as big and ugly as I had imagined.

By her fourth visit, Miss Clews had said I could call her by her first name, which was Janet, and she began to teach me some of the skills that blind people use when getting out and about. These included becoming aware of the surface under my feet so as to distinguish things like concrete, tarmac etc. In addition I learned to listen for traffic as it passed in and out behind bus shelters, even lampposts and stopping at traffic lights. Then there was the sense of smell and I discovered that it was possible to distinguish different shops by their unique aroma. Places like fish and chip shops, chemists, hairdressers and hardware shops were pretty easy even to a novice like me.

After a couple of weeks of training however it was clear to Janet that my confidence was not really increasing to the point where I would attempt to go out unaided. It was at that point that she told me of a new revolutionary mobility technique that had just come in from America for blind people. It was called 'The Long Cane Technique' and they were looking for someone to trial it in the Birmingham area.

I decided somewhat nervously to give it a go, so on her next visit Janet introduced me to Miss Hulme, who I immediately thought was much more vivacious and outgoing than her predecessor. I was told that Miss Hulme was the person who had been chosen to pioneer the Long Cane training in Birmingham and I was thanked for agreeing to be her first pupil.

Miss Hulme (now to be called Mary), full of infectious enthusiasm, went to get the long cane from her car. She actually arrived back with three canes because as I was about to discover, each cane had to be made to measure to suit the needs of each user. I was shocked at how big the canes were, but the requirement was that each cane had to come up to the breastbone of its owner.

"Goodness me", I mused, "If I was ever worried about being self-conscious, then I surely would be with this great thing". Mary soon had me out on my local streets learning the "Long Cane Technique". It was at this time that I started my tradition of naming my sticks. This first one was called "Elsie" for the simple reason that it was a Long Cane (L for long and C for cane – LC, otherwise known as Elsie). Every other long cane I have used since then I have called Elsie.

While I am on this subject I may as well introduce you to the names of my other two sticks. The flimsy symbol cane I spoke about earlier I call Arthur (or more precisely Arfer). This is because one day (many years later and by now more confident) I was running for a bus as I was late for work and using my symbol cane. I arrived at the bus stop, out of breath but just as the bus arrived. I placed my stick on to the platform of the bus at the same moment as a lady jumped on to the bus with all of her weight and snapped my stick in half. I held it up and looked at it rather sorrowfully and said "Oh dear half a stick" and in that moment Arfer was born.

Every symbol cane I have had since then has gone by the same name. More recently I have Eileen. This is what is called a 'Guide Cane'. It is much sturdier than a symbol cane though not quite as long as a "Long Cane". However this guide cane is so strong that I can (and often) do lean on it, hence the name Eileen. Not exactly rocket science, but kids in school (and some child-like adults) love to meet Elsie, Arfer and Eileen.

Anyway, back to long cane training. Mary taught me to hold the cane in the correct way. I am left-handed and have to hold the cane with my left index finger pointed down the flat side of the rubber grip. I then have to hold the cane out in front of my chest and as I walk forward with my left foot I have to swing the cane to the right and then as my right foot goes forward I sweep the cane back to the left with the tip of the cane fractionally above the ground. In this way I am covering the ground where my next footstep is going to be.

This was hard work at first, particularly on the left wrist, however, as I became more confident I was able to relax and when Elsie did locate an object on the pavement I had enough warning to be able to pull up in time and walk around it. It was not long before I was being trained in Birmingham City Centre around the main streets, in and out of new Street Station, up and down the escalators and round the Bull Ring shopping centre.

During this training I did encounter several scary or humorous moments. Just let me tell you of two. I was undertaking a test which involved catching a bus. I was waiting at a bus stop on a busy road near to some traffic lights. It was at a particularly busy time of the day and the traffic kept on stopping near to the bus stop. Anyway I heard what I thought was the bus pull up right by the stop and I attempted to get on. I was waving Elsie around all over the place trying to locate the platform on the bus when eventually Mary, who had been watching me from a short distance away, came up to me and told me I was trying to board a big lorry.

On another occasion Mary had given me an assignment. I had to go into a local shopping centre, about a mile from the training centre, and take a bundle of her washing to the launderette, where she would meet me. I negotiated the bus journey fine and proceeded to the row of shops, somewhat cautiously. I thought to myself that even with my blocked up nasal passages I should be able to sniff out the launderette, no problem at all. Gradually therefore I stepped out with more confidence until I located the smell of the chemist and I knew I was drawing near. Passing the tobacconist, the launderette slowly but surely came into smelling distance. I arrived at where the fragrance of wet washing was particularly strong and turned into the shop. I located the counter, put Mary's bundle of washing there and waited for assistance, or at least to hear the reassuring sound of Mary's "Well done". Instead all I got was a man's deep voice saying, "Can I help you Sir?"

"Yes", I said hesitantly, "I've brought the washing".

"Sorry Sir, you've come to the wrong shop", said the man with what sounded like a smile on his face, "the launderette is next door".

Somewhat embarrassed I left the premises and then arrived safely, but sheepishly at the launderette. Mary was there to greet me and say well done.

"But I blew it", I said.

"No you didn't", replied Mary, "You arrived at the right place, just going via the Midlands Electricity Board, but its mission accomplished and that's what it's all about".

Mary was so positive and encouraging, just what I needed in my life at that particular time. I duly completed my long cane training and because I was one of the first blind people to be trained in this revolutionary new technique I was invited down to London by the BBC to give a demonstration at Broadcasting House and take part in an interview for their radio programme called "In Touch". It was an experience I really enjoyed and that mild flirtation with broadcasting later developed into an affair which has blossomed on and off ever since.

No sooner had I completed my long cane training than news came through that I had to go away from home for three months. Printed indelibly in my memory is the date of 8th June 1967. That was the day when I had to pack up and leave home for the very first time in order to attend the Manor House Rehabilitation Centre in Torquay. I was dreading this day big time. It was so sad saying goodbye to my family, especially Mum. Dad came with me and we boarded the train at New Street Station. I think we sat quietly for most of the journey, which seemed to go on forever. On arriving in Torquay we took a taxi from the station up to the Manor House and I remember feeling like Julie Andrews must have felt in The Sound of Music when she arrived with luggage and guitar in hand at the palatial home of Captain Von Trapp, except I did not have a guitar and I was not about to burst into song.

On entering this mansion of a place we were greeted by one of the administration staff and taken to an office. We were told there would be a meeting for myself and 11 other new entrants at 4pm but for now I would be shown to my room. Dad and I were led up the wide central staircase to the first floor and along a corridor which smelt well-polished and had a wooden floor. Eventually we came to a room on the left and we were shown in. There were four beds and I was told that the other three belonged to Alf (who had been there a couple of weeks), together with Len and Les who were due to be arriving later in the day. I put my bags down on the bed which had been designated for me and Dad helped me unpack. I had a locker and a wardrobe with plenty of drawer space in it. We had been told there would be tea and coffee served downstairs in the lounge so when I had finished unpacking I left the room with Dad, only to bump into a very cheerful sounding guy on the landing outside of the room.

"Hi, nice to meet you, I'm Les" he said in what sounded like a Cockney accent.

We shook hands and I said, "I'm John and this is my Dad".

"Meet my wife", Les said, "This is Jill".

Les turned out to be about 40 years of age. He was from Loughton in Essex. We were destined to become great friends even though of course he was old enough to be my Dad. For the three months I was in Torquay, partially sighted Les always kept a fatherly watch on me and was always chirpy and quick witted.

On my first evening at the Manor House we enjoyed fish and chips for our evening meal in the huge dining room which catered for 72 residents, plus visitors and staff. It was on that first evening too that I encountered the first of many embarrassing moments that I continue to have to this day. I reached out to put salt on my chips only to discover that I had covered them in sugar and had to ask for a replacement meal. Others around the table, except for Dad, laughed at my predicament. The trouble was that I had not yet arrived at the place where I could laugh at myself. That lesson was to come later in the rehabilitation process.

After tea when all of the new residents had arrived there was the traditional weekly barn dance to welcome and help integrate the newcomers. I enjoyed the music and had my introduction to the West Country national anthem *Drink Up Ye Cider* recorded by Adge Cutler and the Wursels, later of course to have a gigantic number one hit record with *I've Got a Brand New Combine Harvester*, It was a good fun way to launch my time in Torquay, but in truth dancing never has been my scene and not that night of all nights.

As the clock ticked around to 10.30 it was time for Dad to leave and go to his hotel for the night. Back in the reception area Dad shook me warmly by the hand and then drew me into a tight hug and I felt him begin to sob in my arms. We both began to cry and through his tears he said, "Good luck son, keep in touch".

It wasn't until this very moment that it dawned on me that Dad loved me, and it was so powerful that I determined to make a success of this course for Mum and Dad's sake as much as my own.

I proceeded to become more competent with my mobility, learn the basics in Braille and typing skills as well as turn my hand to a bit of pottery. A model that I made of a cottage I still have to this day. In terms of developing social skills too we went out to restaurants, discos, dinner-dances, football matches, tenpin bowling and variety shows. It was a great life and a great summer in fact. I grew to love Devon as a county, especially enjoying the seaside resorts of Paignton, Brixham, and Goodrington. I also discovered the very quaint model village at Cockington, where a few years later I would have the thrill of taking my own wife and children, but there was a lot more water to go under the bridge before that point would be reached.

Fear of accidents

I must admit that despite becoming pretty confident in the mobility stakes, I have over the years had my share of accidents. Join with me in a review of some of the more spectacular ones.

I was crossing a road at some traffic lights late one night when a big van swerved around the corner and headed straight for me. The screech of his brakes and the brightness of his headlights full in my face caused me to walk backwards and on impact, the van sent me cart wheeling backwards into the gutter. Thankfully I was only bruised and shaken. After the accident the driver was very caring and considerate, saying that he had not even seen my white stick. He did drive me home once we had both recovered our composure and he later returned to see how I was doing and to invite me to his wedding. Though I was not able to attend, it was certainly the more favourable option, after all it could have been him being invited to my funeral.

On another occasion I was taking my daughter Beverley to nursery. She was just about 4 years of age and walking happily with me hand in hand on my right side. I suddenly became aware that it was very quiet that morning, not the usual chatter of little children talking excitedly with their guardians. I concluded that we must have been a little on the late side, so I did a very irresponsible thing. I folded my stick away (must have been Arthur therefore) and put it in my jacket pocket. I then picked Beverley up in my arms and proceeded to hurry along the pavement the quarter mile or so to the nursery.

However, we had probably only gone about 50 yards when I trod on a mound of earth and disappeared down a six foot hole. Thankfully Beverley fell clear of my arms and landed on the dirt on the other side of the hole, but I went straight down, tearing my jacket and bruising my pride in the process. Quickly one or two of the neighbours had gathered around and were giving Beverley and me a helping hand. Apparently some gas workers had left the hole unattended for a minute or two, just enough time for me to come along and perform one of my stunts! I did later receive some compensation to enable me to buy a new jacket, but I did learn a very painful lesson and thankfully Beverley was not emotionally scarred by the experience.

One dark November night I was returning from London by train to Market Harborough. As the train pulled into Market Harborough railway station I gathered my small suitcase together with a box of literature and records that I had with me. I opened the door and together with my stick and two cases stepped off the train. Through the heavy mist on that winter's night I vaguely heard my wife calling me from the platform, but as I stepped off the train my fall seemed to last for ever and ever. Eventually I hit the ground with a thud and found myself face down on the railway track. I heard my wife screaming, "Are you all right?" in the distance?

Mercifully I was okay, but for a few bruises and a bucket load of embarrassment. I was told later that it was a long train and a short platform but no announcement was made to inform the passengers. Subsequently that was rectified, but I never received an apology.

My final story in this section is also concerning a train. I was travelling into Birmingham to go to work and as the train pulled into Moor Street station I got up from my seat to leave the train as I had done on hundreds of occasions previously. On this occasion however I stepped off the train only for my leading right foot to go down the gap between the train and the platform. My left foot became trapped under the weight of my body and the pain was excruciating. I was very grateful that a young teenage boy, on his way to school was quick of thought to pull me out and get me to a bench. I was in agony and my left ankle had ballooned up to an enormous size. Soon the paramedics had arrived and I was whisked off by ambulance to the City Hospital with a suspected broken ankle. It turned out to be only ligament damage but it was still mighty painful and uncomfortable for many months to come.

In all of these chaotic situations that I have described to you, perhaps with the exception of the van driver, the accidents could have been avoided if I had been using the mobility techniques that I had been taught. The trouble is that when we do anything repetitively and we become good at it, the danger is that we also become somewhat blasé about the whole thing. Somehow that seems to be human nature. I am reminded, not for the first time of some words in the Bible that say 'Pride comes before a fall'. In the Good Book it is also recorded that a man by the name of Job once said, 'That which I feared has come upon me'.

Fear is a powerful force and if we believe in our fears long enough and hard enough then we can bring them into being.

Fear of having to hold on to someone's arm

Strange how some fears that we have can stick around and blight us for life, whilst others are dealt with and overcome at fairly short notice. This fear of having to hold on to someone else's arm when I went out was a very real fear, but it only lasted for a short while

I have already mentioned my love for football in general and for Aston Villa in particular. Well to say I was an avid supporter is a massive understatement. My Dad first took me to the games back in the *Rock Around the Clock* days of 1956, but it was in 1959 that my support of Aston Villa took off big style. In the 1959/60 season under the management of Joe Mercer, Aston Villa went storming to the then League Division 2 championship with some gargantuan performances. And I did not miss a home game all season and even managed a few away games. A most memorable game for me was in November 1959 when Villa beat Charlton Athletic 11-1 at Villa Park. It was a wonderful season but for me it commenced a run where I did not miss a Villa home game for 15 years. It was all nearly so different however.

The last game of football I actually saw perfectly was England's World Cup win against West Germany in July 1966 with the famous Geoff Hurst hat-trick. By the time the new domestic season started at the end of August I can vaguely recall seeing Villa lose 1-0 at home to Arsenal. Even then however there was what I thought was a thick mist in the ground and I could not see the play at the other end of the pitch.

A few weeks later Villa were to play at home to Tottenham Hotspur but by this time I was starting to realise what was happening to my eyes and I decided that I would not attend. However, half hour before kick-off, Brian, a friend from schooldays arrived most unexpectedly and expressed his shock at the news that I was to all intents and purposes, losing my sight. He cajoled me into going to the match and I will always be grateful to Brian for that because not only was it a great match which Villa won 3-2, but I thoroughly enjoyed his highly animated commentary on the game as well as the mutterings of the fans round about me. I was totally persuaded that even losing my eyesight would not keep me away from my beloved Villa Park and so my unbroken record was intact for a few more years yet.

Of course what that did for me also was to break that fear or stigma that I had about having to hold on to someone's arm, particularly a fellow male. After that one game I found other arms to hang on to, including of course my family, and my very good friends Ronnie and Graham to whom I owe a great debt of gratitude for their friendship, particularly during those early traumatic months of going blind. Apart from attending football matches with Ronnie I would also accompany them both to pubs, discos and even the cinema on one occasion.

Ronnie, who had a rugged look with reddish hair was definitely the more macho of my two friends but Graham, with blonde hair and glasses who was nicknamed "The Milky Bar Kid" and "Joe Ninety", was somewhat of a showman. He was into amateur dramatics and it showed whenever we went into a pub or disco with me on his arm, as he liked being the centre of attention when people stared at us. Had I been able to see what was going on I would have cringed with embarrassment, but somehow I was able to enter in to Graham's enjoyment of the whole scene.

Fear of eating in public

From an early age I was a very finicky eater. I was particularly fussy and disparaging about fat on meat, especially boiled ham, bacon or chicken. Likewise with any skin on rice pudding or custard. Then there was the slimy stuff that comes on top of a fried egg, all of these things turned my stomach over. I would make my feelings known to Mum and I often sat at the table picking at my food with 'a face as long as Livery Street', a well-known Birmingham expression for being miserable.

Now with that in mind, can you possibly imagine how nervous I would feel at having a plate of food put in front of me but not being able to see what was on the plate? After all there might be a lump of fat, a piece of skin or something vile to the taste buds, then what about those highly dangerous fish bones? I tell you, eating had suddenly become a very dangerous and scary occupation. Then there was the business of having to eat in public; how daunting was that! Even with my family at first it was a psychological hurdle that had to be overcome. Eventually I think they just got used to me leaving more food on the table and on the floor than went into my mouth. Sometimes I would get so frustrated that I would just pick up the potatoes, meat or vegetables with my fingers.

As is true with many things in life, time is a great healer, for it allows you to adjust to new circumstances. In this case I found that I became more relaxed eating with my family and as they saw me beginning to enjoy my food again, if at times a little ungainly, the more at ease we became with each other. Gradually I grew in confidence to the point whereby I could ask for someone to cut up my meat and roast potatoes, or anything else for that matter which would not fit easily into my mouth.

Okay then that was at home but what about if I was eating out at friends or at a restaurant? Well the same process applied, at first I would struggle and try to manage by myself, often getting into a mess in the process. In that way I would feel embarrassed and so would those eating with me. In the end I came to the realisation that I wanted to enjoy my meal rather than endure it as a trial. Likewise those eating with me also wanted to enjoy their meal and watching me struggle was painful for them. So began a practice that continues to this day in requesting that any awkward items be cut up into bite-sized chunks. Now everyone is more relaxed about it and we can all get on and enjoy what we hope will be an excellent meal.

With normal eyesight of course people make choices based largely on what they can see and that is certainly true of food. When you are without sight you are dependent to a large degree on what other people tell you. There are many occasions when I allow people to make up my mind for me and of course that is not necessarily a good thing, especially from an independence viewpoint. One of those areas for me was food. For instance, people close to me would sometimes say, "You wouldn't like that" and I would just accept it.

One day I was staying with some folk in their house in Devon. On arriving for breakfast, my host said to me, "John, I am terribly sorry but I have run out of breakfast cereals, but I do have some grapefruit."

"That's okay," I said, "I am not much of a breakfast person."

"But I feel really bad about this" replied the lady, "won't you please have some grapefruit?"

"No honestly, I don't like grapefruit" I responded firmly.

Sitting next to me at the table was my blind friend Peter Jackson, a full time Gospel pianist and preacher. Peter, never short of a word or three, entered into the conversation by saying to our concerned host, "Knowing John, he's probably never tried grapefruit."

"That's right, I haven't" came my instant reply.

"Well in that case how do you know you won't like it then?" said Peter, while chuckling at the same time.

I knew I was beginning to lose this little debate as I responded feebly, "Because other people have told me I won't like it".

Now Peter, ever the opportunist to make a spiritual point, came back with, "You are just like the people who say they have no time for Christianity when they have never given Jesus a chance with their lives, It Is nonsensical. Give the grapefruit a try for yourself and then if you don't like it okay, but really it is very refreshing."

"Will you have some then John?" said our kind host who had been an amused bystander to this light-hearted discussion.

"Yes, okay then, but just a little" I said, with Peter choking back the giggles at my side.

Well, as you will probably realise by now, although the grapefruit tingled initially on my tongue, I have to confess that it was not anywhere near as sour as I had been led to believe, in fact it was rather nice and as Peter had rightly said, very refreshing. Now I love grapefruit, but to think of all those years I missed out just because I was allowing myself to be controlled by other people's ideas and opinions instead of looking into it for myself so that I could make an informed judgement. Oh yes and Peter was correct in his comment that many people do make the same mistake when it comes to the big questions in life. We often mimic other people's opinions or experiences instead of doing some research and finding out for ourselves. I still think one of the most important questions is "Where will I go when I die?" or "Is there such a place as Heaven or Hell and if so how do I get to one and avoid the other?" I have always felt that these are important questions to be asking and that unlike the grapefruit, which is far more trivial (sorry grapefruit worshippers) the matter of life, death and eternity are far too important for me to rely on someone else's opinions. I have to know for myself.

Now for me eating is an adventure. My outlook has totally changed and far from being ruled by fear, I am now excited by the anticipation of what might be on the end of my fork or spoon.

Fear of not working again

To be truthful this was more of a lingering negative thought than an outright fear because there were other things much more pressing at the time. However, as I became more used to life as a blind person I realised, particularly in the late 1960s, there were not that many job opportunities available to people with sight loss. If I said to you basketwork, light engineering, typing, telephony, physiotherapy and computer programming then that is a comprehensive list of what was available. The first two on the list were probably the most common and the last two the most exclusive. My early interest in computer programming was because I used to enjoy working out logical mathematical problems in my head and I thought that would be a prime requisite for a computer programmer. I had not taken into consideration the need to be a proficient Braille reader.

It was at Torquay however, during my three months of rehabilitation that I really took to the typewriter keyboard and discovered just how much I enjoyed communicating in that way. I sent letters home to the family fairly frequently and found it to be a great and therapeutic way of expressing my feelings. Having shown such an aptitude in this way it was no surprise that I was recommended to undertake further training in London at a commercial college for the blind to be trained as an audio typist.

At first I felt insulted by this assessment because the only typists I had ever come across were women. Apart from my fears of that particular species there was the nagging thought that this was a particularly effeminate job for a man to have to undertake. Ultimately I did commence training on 1st January 1968 at

Pembridge Place near Notting Hill Gate and for the next eight months that was to be my home. Whilst there I made some really great friendships, one of which has lasted to this day.

On my very first day I was gingerly climbing the stairs to get to my second floor bedroom, which I was to share with three other lads. I was partway up the second flight of stairs when I collided head on with someone much more robust than me and I fell backwards down the flight of stairs. As had always been my way, I said quickly, "Sorry mate".

"That's okay, it was probably my fault", replied the man I was to come to know as Neville, in his broad Norfolk accent.

It turned out that Neville was sharing a room just across the landing from me. As we got to know each other it transpired that he was suffering from a similar eye condition to myself, we shared a love for sport and like me he had been a keen listener to pirate radio stations.

Following on from Torquay this was my second time away from home and just as I had enjoyed my three months in sunny Devon I also had a wonderful time in London. I made some really good friendships and the food at the college was excellent.

Whilst thinking about my time at Pembridge I would like to share with you two other events that occurred. Firstly, it was June and I had returned home to Birmingham by train for the weekend. On travelling back to London on the Sunday teatime it was really hot with temperatures in the high 80s Fahrenheit. I arrived back at the college to discover that most of the residential students had disappeared off to the King George VI pub on the Bayswater Road, a regular haunt for quite a few of them. I was not a habitual pub goer, but on that hot and steamy night I headed off there in search of some much needed liquid refreshment. I was about to have a rude awakening in more senses than one however.

It was about 8pm as I entered the packed oldie-worldy pub and on entering the lounge area headed off to the right-hand side where I knew that the blind and partially sighted contingent gathered. Amid the noisy chatter somehow I picked up the sound of a voice I recognised. It was Frank, a man with a very posh English speaking voice, kind of a Hugh Grant type, 30 years before his time. Frank was in his late 30's, quite a bit older than most of us at the college.

"Frank is that you?" I called knowing very well it was of course.

"Ah John my boy", he replied as if he was really glad to see me, "Chris is up at the bar if you want me to take you up to place your order."

Frank did have some sight and so I accepted his offer to weave me through the crowd up to the bar.

"Flanner's back and he's gasping for a drink" said Frank once he had located Chris, still waiting patiently to be served.

Chris broke off from a conversation he was having and turned to me saying, "John I would like you to meet Julie".

"So you're John", the lady chipped in.

"Yes" I said "and you are Julie?"

"Of course" she responded in a rather beguiling tone, "I've not seen you here before."

"I've only been here twice previously and never on a Sunday" I said somewhat nervously.

"What are you drinking?" she asked and I replied, "I'll have a shandy".

Julie expressed some surprise that I was not drinking anything stronger than shandy but I explained that I was very thirsty, especially after a long, hot train journey and I wanted a long thirst-quenching drink.

Chris, still at the bar, piped up, "He likes rum and coke as well though".

With that Julie said, "George, get my friend John a pint of bitter shandy and a large rum and coke on me".

Out of courtesy more than anything else I stood at the bar with Chris and Julie together with her friend George who by now had made himself known to me. I remember thinking to myself, "She might be old enough to be my mother, or maybe not", when she flawed me with a question.

"What do you think I look like John?" she asked.

Somewhat flustered by the question from someone I had only met a minute or two previously and wanting to be complimentary to the mystery woman who had bought me a couple of drinks I said, "I think you are a cross between Sophia Loren and Elizabeth Taylor."

Seizing her moment and my free hand she said "You are not far wrong, just feel that" as she slapped my hand on one of her ample breasts.

In a state of shock I pulled my hand away as if I had touched a live electric fence, spilling some of my drink in the process. It was a hot evening anyway but now I was sweltering and my heart was thumping full of nervous energy.

Julie proceeded to tell me how much she liked me and would love it if I would agree to go round to her flat in Bayswater one evening.

George, with his strong Cockney accent, chipped in at this point, He won't come, he is chicken, and after all he is only a boy.

"Of course he'll come, won't you John" said Julie In what I now realised was a well-rehearsed routine.

Whilst having no intention of ever meeting Julie again or going within a half mile radius of that pub, I did say that I would meet Julie there at 7.30pm the following Wednesday. As we parted and I left with Chris to go to our table Julie shouted somewhat assertively, "Don't let me down now."

I arrived at the large oval shaped oak table where my fellow students were sitting and there was much hilarious laughter and jibing at my expense. I hastily finished my shandy and my rum and coke and left the pub with Frank. As we walked back the short distance to college Frank was keen to know if I was going to take Julie up on her offer. Despite my insistence that in no way was I going to do so, Frank tried everything in his power to persuade me that this would be good for my manhood. However, I was scared and did not mind admitting it. Exasperated with me, Frank eventually said that if I did not turn up for the date then he would go in my place, which incidentally, is exactly what happened. You can probably guess the result and as I understand it, a good time was had by all, except that the night out at Julie's place, cost Frank a fair few quid.

The next incident of note took place in the classroom one day while we were waiting for our typing teacher to arrive. There were only four of us to a class and my friend Chris used to sit behind me. Chris had been blind from birth, he was the same age as me, short of stature, liked his beer and had a great sense of humour. Like me he gave a name to his cane, he said he had had the same long cane for years, however because he was very short so was his cane, he named it Arthur Conley after the diminutive soul singer of Sweet Soul Music fame.

While in the classroom Chris and I had been given a toffee by Barbara, the only female student out of the four of us. Still waiting for our teacher Mrs Craig to arrive, I unwrapped my toffee and put it in my mouth. I then screwed up the paper and threw it back over my head hoping to hit Chris on some part of his anatomy. At that moment Mrs Craig walked in and thankfully did not see my uncharacteristically loutish behaviour. We proceeded through our typing lesson during which we had to type out some audio dictation which lasted for about 20 minutes. At the end of the class we left our work on Mrs Craig's desk and went off for our tea break.

On returning to the class for the continuation of the lesson Mrs Craig, a 60 year old disciplinarian of the old school, began by saying that on the whole the work was of a very high standard, with the exception of Chris, whose two sheets of paper were totally blank. When she walked over to Chris' Olympia typewriter, she was able to see the reason why. A piece of toffee wrapping paper had become lodged on the roller where the typewriter keys would make contact. I knew that Chris was about to be lambasted for his apparent foolishness and so with trepidation I had to own up to the fact that I had thrown the toffee paper. Mrs Craig expressed surprise and disappointment at my action and both Chris and I were in for detention that night to undertake the work again. Thankfully Chris did not hold that against me and neither did Mrs Craig who went on to be instrumental in helping me make the most important decision of my life, but more of that later.

I went on to leave the college gaining Distinctions in RSA Audio Typing Elementary and Intermediate levels. By this time I was really enjoying living away from home and I wanted to stay working in London. So it was that I secured a position as an audio typist with the Ministry of Overseas Development in Clerkenwell. Subsequently I have gone on to work for over 20 years performing the same typing role for the Inland Revenue. It is a job that I have really enjoyed, meeting some fantastic people in the process, even women and do you know what, they are not nearly as frightening as I made them out to be, apart from one or two glaring exceptions that is. So as far as never working again is concerned, I need not have had any worries at all.

Fear of being alone

As a teenager I became an avid cinemagoer, often going alone to a variety of the many cinemas in our locality as well as in the Birmingham city centre. One Sunday afternoon when I was about 15 years of age I took myself off into Birmingham to the Odeon in New Street for the opening day showing of *The Young Ones* starring Cliff Richard and The Shadows. I was a big fan of theirs and I had already bought the single of the same name which had shot to the top of the charts. In the film there is a scene where Cliff is walking on a beach with his girlfriend and as they walk in and out of the many children playing and building sandcastles, Cliff is singing the title song. Contained within the song is the lyric

...and some day when the years have flown / darling then we'll teach the young ones of our own.

Being a sensitive and sentimental kid, it brought a lump to my throat and a desire arose within me, one day that might be me, but somehow I doubted that I would ever be that lucky.

As I got older and my fear of girls intensified the dream seemed to drift off almost into oblivion. As I have said in a much earlier passage it was not that I did not like the look of girls, on the contrary, I found many of them really attractive and appealing to the eye. It was just that I never had the courage to actually make a date. Fear of rejection, which I perhaps should have included within this list of fears, was perhaps the overriding factor. Then of course going blind just capped it as far as I was concerned, for what girl in her right mind would ever want to go out with a blind person?

One Friday night in December of 1968 I was travelling back from London to Birmingham for the weekend on the Midland Red bus. The purpose of my visit as well as to see my family was of course to watch Aston Villa play. However on the journey as we meandered slowly through the streets of London, my thoughts turned to the matter of, "Will I ever get a girlfriend?"

As I turned this matter back and forth inside my head, I felt an aching within my heart. After all I was 21 years of age and never had what you would call a real girlfriend. I had been out a couple of times with Pamela, a girl from Dunlop who I had liked very much, but in truth she really had her heart set on a disc jockey friend of hers and she just liked me as a friend and I did start going out with a blind girl from Pembridge, but I always felt ill at ease with myself when we were together.

Now on the coach, however, as we sped up the motorway I had this intense longing for a steady girlfriend. A few weeks earlier I had become a 'born again' Christian while attending Westminster Chapel (of which more later) and I was still having some struggles concerning that whole experience. In that moment of agonising on the bus I found myself mouthing a prayer from deep within my heart.

"Oh God if you are real and you have come to live inside me then would you please give me a girlfriend."

Prayer uttered, my mind came to rest and I enjoyed the remainder of the journey. Roughly two weeks later I was back in Birmingham again for yet another football match. On the Saturday night of 28th December 1968 my Mum and Dad had gone to a local pub called The College Arms where they used to have a bit of a sing-along and I joined them there for the night. My sister Joan also came along as did her friend from work Sylvia with her fiancé. We had been there for about an hour and the singing was getting into full swing as the alcohol took effect. More importantly for Dad and me, however, was that a man selling all kinds of seafood, for which we were suckers, had entered the pub. Dad and I had a bag of cockles each whilst Mum preferred the mussels. Politely I offered my cockles around. In fact Sylvia was sat on my right and I give you my word that all I said to her that night in the pub was "Would you like a cockle?"

She replied with a firm, "No thank you", ending the conversation before it got started, but little did she know that she was destined to become my wife.

That night at the College Arms was most enjoyable and we left at about 11pm, but not before Dad had invited a crowd of people back to the house for a bit of a party. Dad, who often played the piano at the local pub, only needed a few beers to get him in the party mood and about a dozen people came back to my parent's home that night. I quickly volunteered to sit in the corner of the long, rectangular living room by the record player with my beloved large collection of singles. In those days I had Braille labels on most of my singles so I was able to find exactly the right discs.

After the party had been under way for a while, my sister Joan, came over to me and said, “Would you play something especially for my friend Sylvie as she is desperately unhappy with her boyfriend. One of her favourite artists is Otis Redding”.

I quickly searched through my collection which was all strictly in alphabetical order, until I came to the Otis Redding section. I picked one out and shouted above the din of lively conversation, “This is *Mr Pitiful* by Otis Redding especially for Sylvia”.

The record had hardly started to get into full swing when Sylvia came across and said, “How did you know that is one of my favourite songs? Thank you, would you like to dance?”

I could hardly believe my ears and before I could take it in, this young woman who had earlier refused my offer of a cockle, was taking me by the hand and leading me around the dimly lit living room in a bit of a slow dance. She held me close and I loved it, I felt a little awkward in terms of the dancing (if that is what it was) but I sure did feel good and I just did not want Otis to stop singing. Feeling Sylvia’s body next to mine was sensational, I felt so amazingly proud and chuffed with myself. All too soon the record stopped and I had to get back to my duties of playing the music, however my night had been made and I would cherish that moment for the rest of my life.

On Monday I was back at work typing away for the Ministry of Overseas Development at their Clerkenwell office in London. From time to time during the day my mind would drift back to that Saturday night and the slow dance inspired by Otis Redding who was now more of a hero than ever.

After work I travelled by bus as usual back to my digs in Stoke Newington. Smalley Road was located in a fairly run down working class area but the home in which I lived was warm and friendly, Ron and Rose saw to that. They were a really lovely, jovial couple and were parents to Mike, one of my room-mates from Pembridge. We had struck up a good friendship at college and when Mike knew I was planning to stay in London to work he told his parents and they immediately offered me a room in their home. Mike himself was a great character. A year younger than me, Mike had been blinded by a firework at the age of 10 yet was always the life and soul of the party. He left college as a fully trained shorthand typist and obtained a job at what was then called the Board of Trade.

Not surprisingly Mike did not stay there too long before he went on to further studies and qualified as a Social Worker, where he quickly rose up the promotional ladder. A keen sportsman, Mike also went on to represent the UK in athletics, skiing and what is called blind cricket involving ball bearings inside of the larger than normal ball so that the batsman can hear where the ball is pitching. In the early 1980s Mike was the subject of *This Is Your Life*, still presented in those days by the great Irish broadcaster, Eamonn Andrews. My wife and I were privileged to be in the audience as guests that night. Mike, I understand, has more recently been part of the Committee that has successfully campaigned to bring the 2012 Olympic Games to London, thus resulting in him being honoured with an OBE.

Anyway, I was relaxing back in my room at Smalley Road, listening to The Archers as I did in those days, when Rose shouted up the stairs, "John, there's a phone call for you".

I leapt off the bed and hurried down the winding staircase. I picked up the phone to find that it was my sister Joan on the phone.

"Hello John, sorry to bother you, but you made quite a hit at the weekend" she said with some amusement in her voice.

"In what way?" I replied coyly.

"With Sylvia of course and she's written you a letter, which she wants me to read to you over the phone" said Joan sounding just a little excited.

Of course I could not wait to hear what Sylvia had to say knowing from Joan's comments that it was going to be favourable. Joan read the letter to me and in essence Sylvia was saying that she was desperately unhappy and locked into a relationship with her fiancé in which she felt trapped. She said that she enjoyed meeting me and would love to meet up again for a chat. Once again I could hardly believe my ears, a girl, a member of the opposite sex no less, was asking to meet with me. This was unheard of, but I was up for it. My only concern though was this boyfriend, what about him?

Next morning I got into work extra early so that I could type Sylvia a letter via my sister. I arranged to meet her the following Friday, saying that my coach would be arriving at Birmingham Digbeth Coach Station at around 8.30pm. If she was there to meet me then we could go for a drink and a chat somewhere.

The week flew by and in no time at all I was getting off the coach in Birmingham and there was Sylvia to meet me. We walked hand in hand through Birmingham city centre and it felt so natural. As we talked there was more time to take things in now and whilst I was 5ft 10ins tall and very skinny at just 9st, Sylvia was about 5ft 3ins and a little under 9st. I later discovered that she had short, light brown hair and big sparkling brown eyes.

We jumped on the number 5 bus from Corporation Street and headed back to my parent's home in Erdington. We then headed off across the road to our local pub, 'The Chase' where we chatted at great length for an hour or so before it was time for Sylvia to go home. We talked about a number of things but in the main it centred on how unhappy she was because she was experiencing a certain amount of abuse at the hands of her boyfriend and that she needed to summon up the courage to put an end to the relationship.

I am glad to say that in the following week when I was back in London, I received a phone call from Sylvia to say that she had made it clear to Kenny that she did not love him and that their relationship was over. I breathed a sigh of relief and congratulated Sylvia for having the courage to do what must have been a very difficult thing.

"I'll see you on Friday at the same time then" I said.

"Yes, of course, I can't wait" responded Sylvia enthusiastically.

It was beginning to look to me as if my heartfelt prayer uttered on the Midland Red coach just a few weeks beforehand had been answered in spectacular fashion. I remember on my way to work the next morning saying, "Thank you God for answering my prayer in such a surprising way". I think this was the first time that I became aware that God is the God of surprises. I have benefited from many of his surprises since.

Following our first meeting I was in Birmingham every weekend but I have to confess that it was only four weeks after our first meeting that I did something totally out of character for me at that time. We had started attending a Saturday night disco held at a club called The Heartbeat which was located on the same complex as the Silver Blades Ice Rink and Bowling Alley in the centre of Birmingham. We loved the music which was played there, which was mainly soul and Tamla Motown with a few chart songs thrown in for good measure. We danced a little, clumsily in my case, and talked a lot.

On the night of 25th January 1969, as we were sat talking and sipping our drinks with *Ob-La-Di Ob-La-Da* by Marmalade playing in the background, I found myself saying;

"Sylvia, I love you so much, will you marry me?"

I was shocked at the words coming out of my mouth, but even more shocked when Sylvia said,

"Yes I will, of course I will".

Wow! Could it really be that after four weeks and four dates with my first girlfriend I was now about to become engaged to be married? Following that, Sylvia and I enjoyed a very pleasant courtship, actually waiting until the June to become officially engaged and then getting married at St Margaret's Church, Erdington, Birmingham on 29th November 1969, just 11 months after our first meeting in the College Arms. The original idea was to get married the following year, but to be perfectly honest we could not wait for that.

The night before the wedding Sylvia spent a quiet evening at home with family. However I went to a favourite local pub called The Lyndhurst, mainly because I liked the band that played there at weekends with their mix of Irish, country and western and pop music. It was just a few mates and me having a nice time, but what I didn't know was that they were getting me slowly blotto by doing things to my drinks, i.e. if I asked for a rum and coke, they would make it a double rum and so on. When the pub closed I thought I was going home, but I remember going through a turnstile and thinking in my semi-drunken state, "I must be at the Villa".

I then found myself standing next to a load of people, probably all men, who were cheering and applauding. Then came the shouts of "Off, off, off". Yes, you've probably guessed it, I was at a strip club. Now I ask you, fancy taking a blind man to a strip club!

Miraculously I awoke on my wedding day with no hangover but loads of nerves. The wedding was set for the hallowed hour of 3pm, just at the time Villa was due to kick off. It was bitterly cold and icy that November morning however and there was still snow on the ground from an earlier snowfall so the match just might be called off...the football match that is, not the wedding! I had made myself unpopular with a number of people for arranging the wedding to coincide with a Villa home match, not least Reverend Power, because he too was a Villa fan.

The wedding service itself was a pretty traditional affair. Sylvia looked lovely in the white dress that she had hired from Young's Hire Service and she had four bridesmaids, her sisters Linda and Joyce and my two sisters Joan and Susan. We had three hymns, all of which we knew from school assembly days including *Immortal Invisible God only Wise, Love Divine all Loves Excelling* and *The Lord's My Shepherd*. You'll be glad to know also that when Sylvia arrived at the front of the Church to join me in my light grey suit, just before the Vicar said "Dearly beloved we are gathered here today in the sight of God...", he whispered to me "Good news John, the match has been postponed" and from that moment on I knew this was going to be a good day.

Heaven for me arrived at 6pm when Graham (alias the Milky Bar Kid or Joe Ninety) drove us into Birmingham to catch our train. Sitting on that railway carriage with my bride was indeed one of the very proudest moments in my life. I really never thought it would happen to me but it had.

So that was the fear of never getting married over and done with you might say but what about the fear of never having children? After about a year of married bliss, with one or two exceptions of course for we are only human after all, Sylvia was feeling that she would love to have a baby. If I am honest I did not really want a child coming along and disturbing what was now a very pleasant way of life. By this time it had been a good 18 months or so since I had moved back from London to get a job working as an audio typist at the Inland Revenue, Birmingham 16 Tax District as it was then at King Edward House, New Street, Birmingham. Sylvia, somewhat coincidentally was then working at Dunlop as a cashier in the staff canteen. Eventually, however, as men tend to do, I relented and as a first wedding anniversary present we decided that we would start trying for our first child.

In the spring of 1971 I returned home from work one night to an empty flat. Sylvia had gone to see the doctor as she had not been feeling at all well and as she had already missed one period we were thinking she just might be pregnant. I had been home from work for about half an hour or so when the doorbell rang and I went to open the front door.

Sylvia was there, she flung her arms around me and said, "Congratulations, you've done it. We're going to have a baby".

I was so amazed and excited, I embraced Sylvia in a tight bear hug and swung her around with glee. Another one of those proud, chest-expanding moments for me and my confidence levels rose dramatically and possibly went way off the scale. Our beautiful daughter, Beverley Jane was born on 8 October 1971 at Birmingham's Dudley Road Hospital weighing in at 7lbs. She was born on a Friday night after Sylvia had endured a long labour and I was honoured to be present at the birth to witness this miracle of creation.

God really does have a sense of humour because he was beginning to deal with my fear of girls and not having children in an amazing way. Having Beverley around was wonderful, however, something extraordinary and deeply challenging was about to break forth in our lives. It was now February 1972 and Beverley was just 4 months old. I was busy typing in my Birmingham office when a lady popped her head around the door and said, "John, there's a phone call for you in the main office."

Why the call had come through in the main Pay As You Earn Office I never did find out. However, on answering the phone I was surprised to find that it was Sylvia on the other end of the line and her tone immediately told me that she was not at all happy.

"John, you are never going to believe this, but I am pregnant again." There seemed like an eternal silence before she went on more forcibly, "You and your bright ideas. I am so embarrassed." With that she broke down in tears and conscious of many colleagues around me I just said that I would come home early so that we could talk and Sylvia put the phone down.

As I walked back to my office I tried to look calm, but really I was trembling inside. "How could this be?" I thought to myself.

On the way back to my office I stopped off at the gents in an attempt to recover my composure and reflected, "Malcolm Muggeridge, it's all his fault, if only I had not listened to him."

At this time in our lives Sylvia and I were still very young and immature as Christians and seeking to grow in our understanding of the faith and in obedience to God's word, the Bible. We were attending St Martin's Church, a notable edifice, located in Birmingham's Bull ring. We used to attend the Sunday morning and evening services there, but since the arrival of our baby daughter we only went in the morning. On Sunday evenings BBC television were conducting a series of debates on the rights and wrongs of birth control for the Christian. We watched the anti-birth control debate presented by Malcolm Muggeridge a highly respected writer and broadcaster well known for his conversion to Christianity from atheism late on in his life. We had heard him preach at St Martin's Church and been very impressed. We were equally impressed by his anti-birth control stance too and we decided (or was it I decided?) that we would now live and make love by faith, using the self-control method. Great idea in theory as we truly wanted to honour God in all areas of life, but now we were expecting another child so soon after the joy of welcoming Beverley into the world.

As the months passed by we moved from our 15th floor Council flat to a first floor three bedroom maisonette near to where my parents lived and in fact where I had lived since the age of 11. We also changed to attending a more local church, this time a lively Pentecostal Church that had been recommended to us by a friend. Each Friday night we would have a crowd of teenagers come to our house, mainly friends of my brother Paul who himself was a lively 17 year old at the time. These kids, usually numbering between 20 and 30, would come with their musical instruments and we would sing modern Gospel songs, pray and read the Bible together.

One Friday night in August of that year, when Sylvia was coming up to eight months pregnant, we were having such a meeting and singing heartily. During one of the songs Sylvia turned to me and said, "I have a pain in my back and don't feel well. I am going to bed to have a lie down. Tell the kids the refreshments are all out in the kitchen."

Sylvia made her exit and a few minutes later I went up to see how she was. Seeing that she was clearly in a lot of discomfort I did not know quite what to do. She had been to see the Doctor earlier that afternoon and he had done some poking and prodding around so maybe the baby was lying on a nerve, we just did not know what to think.

Eventually it was decided that I should call the midwife who quickly arrived and ascertained that Sylvia had actually gone into labour. The midwife, named Pat, normally a very pleasant young lady, was not at all amused by the number of people in our home and in no uncertain terms she told me to clear the house because this was no kind of atmosphere in which to give birth.

I hastily obeyed my orders and the youth meeting came to an abrupt end, but not until they had insisted on saying a prayer for Sylvia. After making some preliminary arrangements, the midwife undertook a more thorough examination of Sylvia's anatomy and exclaimed, "Has Dr Griffiths said anything about twins?"

A startled Sylvia said, "No, only that I have a big baby".

"Well I'm not convinced," responded Pat, "I'm sure I can feel several arms and legs in there. I know we agreed that you could have this baby at home, but to be on the safe side I am going to ring for an ambulance".

Well the midwife's concerns had certainly raised our anxiety levels and as Sylvia continued further on into labour, my Mum and Sister Susan arrived from the maisonette just below ours. By now the whisper had gone around that we just might be having twins. For some strange reason the ambulance took ages to arrive and by the time it did get to us Sylvia's labour had advanced to the point of no return and she was just about to give birth. I was waiting anxiously outside the bedroom door sitting on the stairs with Mum when suddenly I heard a baby's faint cry and without ado the midwife had opened the door and thrust this baby into my arms and said, "Congratulations, it's a girl. Everything is fine, she has all her bits, but as I suspected there is another baby on the way".

By now I was in a daze as I held our new baby daughter who was born at 11.50pm. Now the race was on to see whether the other baby would be born the same side of midnight.

Beverley was sleeping soundly through all the commotion, Mum was making the ambulance crew a cup of tea downstairs and Dr Griffiths was just entering the house as the second baby arrived, another daughter at 12.10am. It was an identical twin, born on a different day. Unlike giving birth less than a year ago to Beverley, Sylvia's comment this time was that it was easy, just like shelling peas. The twins were born six weeks or so premature but just 10 months and 10 days after the arrival of Beverley.

Dr Griffiths sat for a few moments at the foot of Sylvia's bed and bemoaned the fact that he had once again just missed the birth of twins. He expressed his surprise at it being more than one child and remarked, "I bet you have not got two lots of names chosen".

"No" I said, "we only have Allison Marie".

Dr Griffiths thought for a moment and said, "I know it's none of my business, but maybe you should name the second baby Allison Marie as she was born after midnight and her initials are AM".

Well that really appealed to my mind and so I quickly obtained Sylvia's agreement, who was weary and in no state to debate the issue. Dr Griffiths and I then went through the process of trying to find names with the initials PM for the first-born twin. After a while I had to confess, with the occasional nod of approval from my very tired wife, that the only name that really appealed to us was Sara Louise and so we settled on that.

Because the babies were born premature they had to be taken off to Sorrento Maternity Hospital in Birmingham to be cared for and it was quite emotional for us, especially for Sylvia, to let Sara and Allison go after all the hard work and emotion of the evening. She found it very upsetting to think that these two beautiful identical babies were being taken away so soon and in particular that we had only one carry cot for them. This had taken us and the medical profession by surprise. To add to the sense of anti-climax that Sylvia was feeling, not only had her precious new born babies been taken away for a while, but at about 1am the local fish and chip shop was closed and she really fancied tucking into roe and chips.

Not many people can claim that Malcolm Muggeridge had a hand in the conception of their twins, and we had certainly not made a conscious decision to have a baby quite so soon the second time around. Nevertheless I truly believe that God himself decreed and purposed the birth of Sara and Allison and together with our son Ian who came along six years later, no four children could be loved by their parents any more than ours. There have been tests and trials along the way as well as much joy and I thank God for these wonderful gifts that he saw fit to entrust into our care. I just hope we have done a half decent job in parenting them the way our Heavenly Father would want.

I never thought that this could happen to me, but it did and to date Sylvia and I also have nine young grandchildren in our beautiful family.

Section Two – FUN

I love the Beach Boys hit song *Fun, Fun, Fun.* Somehow for me it captures the essence of fun with it being so light of spirit and conveying a glorious freedom and the feeling that all is well with the world. Maybe other songs, movies or situations do the same for you, but deep down fun really is important. If you take fun out of your world for any length of time then life will become really irksome.

Amidst all of the fears already outlined there were also of course times of fun such as going on family holidays to Blackpool, playing and watching sport, going to the cinema or watching a favourite television programme. Fun, however, only became an integral part of my life after losing my sight and in this section I want to share with you some of the experiences that have made me and others laugh, often at my own expense.

Bowled over

One of the most profound and lasting influences in my life took place within the first week of me arriving at the Manor House in Torquay for my three months of rehabilitation. Brian Varley, a stocky, muscular man, was a member of the staff and it was his job to provide us with a series of social events that would help towards developing our social skills which, certainly in my case, had been crushed by the onset of blindness.

My first sortie with Brian was to be taken by mini bus with five others to a bowling alley in Torquay town centre. When I could see I loved tenpin bowling and indeed used to bowl for a team in a league; we were called The Kinksmen, named after the 60s pop group The Kinks. However I could not see the point of going bowling as a blind person when you would not have the thrill of seeing the pins go down. Perhaps nearer to the mark would be to say that I did not want to go through the embarrassment of bowling the ball down the gutter, or even worse down the wrong lane.

On the evening that we went to the alley it was mercifully fairly quiet and it was not long before the six of us, fully equipped in our bowling shoes were busy choosing the most comfortable balls and then taking our seats ready for the first assault on the pins. Usually when people are excited about something they can't wait to get started and even adults in a childlike kind of a way will shout out, "Can I go first?"

On this occasion, however someone piped up "Can I go last?"

That was soon followed by someone else saying, "No it's all right, I'll go last."

As for me, I most definitely wanted to go last!

Eventually we were all somewhat stunned when this bloke called Geoff interjected to say, "Okay guys, I'll go first".

We were all very relieved and as Geoff picked up his ball and stepped back we were all ears. There was a hush around the lane as Geoff moved forward to bowl, with me at least hoping his ball went down the gutter. After all there would be nothing to live up to then would there?

Suddenly Geoff gave out a loud shriek of anguish and almost as one we said, "What's the matter Geoff, have you fallen?"

"No, but one of my eyes has fallen out," came his reply, "and I think it's gone rolling down the alley".

This was my introduction to the world of artificial eyes and I have had quite a few encounters since then, but at that moment none of us knew whether to laugh or cry. There was a long, awkward silence which was shattered when Geoff with impeccable timing said "But don't worry chaps, I'll be okay once I get my eye in."

At that moment we all broke into spontaneous laughter, and something broke in me that day as I laughed so much that tears ran down my face. I recall on several occasions throughout the evening I would just break out into laughter as I recalled Geoff's comments.

I reflected on the events, "Here is Geoff, scarred from an explosion at work, no real eyes and yet he is able to laugh at himself and seemingly enjoy having other people have a laugh at his expense. This was a liberating experience for me and from that moment on I know I began to loosen up and not take myself nearly so seriously. I heard that Geoff had died a few years later, still only a young man, but he will always be a hero to me for that priceless lesson he taught me at the bowling alley in the heart of Torquay.

Many years later I was at a bowling alley in Birmingham with my son Ian. It was a Saturday morning and fairly hectic with lots of children of all ages playing, especially in junior league bowling. Ian and I were sent off to play on lane number one, which I thought was great because it meant that we had a wall on our left and lane two on our right. Sometimes when people are bowling either side I find it distracts my concentration. On this occasion however we were in a quiet little corner and as it turned out, it was a good job that we were.

Ian bowled first and true to form he got a strike with his first ball. Now it was my turn. I stepped back and concentrated hard before stepping forward with the ball in my left hand as usual. As I approached the lane and was about to release the ball I was filled with a deep sense of panic because I sensed something in my way, but it was too late and I let the ball go with all of its usual force on its way to get me a strike, or so I hoped. However, the ball had hardly left my hand when I heard a terrific noise of the ball crashing against metal and other things. Ian rushed up to me in a flash, but before he could speak, full of concern I said, "What have I done?"

"Dad you turned on an angle and bowled the ball across the lane, it bounced against the left edge of the gutter, hit the wall, made a hole in it and it has gone straight through" said Ian with a great deal of alarm in his voice. Ian continued, "What are we going to do now?"

"Let's carry on as if nothing has happened", I suggested.

Exasperated Ian said, "You must be joking, loads of people heard the bang and they are staring at the hole in the wall."

"Keep your voice down" I said to Ian, "I just want to carry on as normal."

"But Dad you don't understand", Ian protested, "people are watching and I think you should go to reception and see what they have to say."

After a few minutes I was able to persuade Ian to get on with the game on the understanding that at the end I would go and as it were "confess my sins". To this day I really do not know what it was that made me go off at an angle like that. I did however go and explain to the lady on reception at the end. Thankfully she made light of it, said it was only plywood and we actually watched as an engineer who maintains the lanes, clambered inside the hole and retrieved the ball. We did return to the alley about six months later for a more conventional game of bowling and would you believe it, the hole was still there having not been repaired.

Washed up

One of the many hard things I find as a blind person and particularly as a husband is that there are lots of things I cannot do that bring extra pressure and responsibility on to my wife and sometimes children. For instance I cannot do the painting and decorating, I cannot drive the car, read or fill in the many forms that come through the post. I did try mowing the lawn, but my career as a would-be gardener came to an abrupt end when I took the electric mower straight over the cable, completely cutting it into two. Mercifully I didn't even get an electric shock, but it was still a shock if you know what I mean and enough of one for me not to be allowed near the mower ever again.

One job I did take to however was doing the washing up. I was drawn to this task particularly when our three daughters were very small. It was about 6pm one evening and tea was just about over and done with. As anyone who has ever had children will know, the time leading up to bedtime can be very stressful with small children. At about 4pm they start to get tired, grizzly and argumentative. By this time too parents are weary themselves and desperately trying to come up with ideas to keep their little angels awake until bedtime rolls around at about 7 o'clock. Bath time is a godsend because the kids usually have a bit of fun splashing around with their toys in the water and it does seem to revive them for a while, but in truth it is very hard work trying to keep them amused and in a good frame of mind. The favourite television programme, a singsong or reading them a story often provide short-term relief. Anyway it was into one of those scenarios that on one night I actually volunteered to go into the kitchen and perform the washing up duties.

I left Sylvia to oversee the bath rota whilst I disappeared into the kitchen to commence my labour of love. I must have done a good job because this quickly became an acceptable pattern and to be fair it was a job that on the whole I really enjoyed. There is no doubt that I got some personal satisfaction from actually doing a job well in the knowledge that it was one task that I was saving Sylvia from doing.

To this day I can often be found at the kitchen sink either listening to the radio or more often than not singing away to myself. I have come a long way since those days, miming the hymns in school assembly and now I am just happy to make a joyful noise. We used to have a small poster above our kitchen sink which read 'Divine worship takes place here three times daily'.

One night, however, things did not go according to plan at the kitchen sink. I was there singing away to myself working in my regular routine of taking the dirty dishes from the left, putting them into the washing up bowl and then putting them to drain on the right side to dry off. As I was scouring a saucepan I became aware of bits of food floating around in the water. I picked a couple of lumps out of the water and began to squeeze them. I held them up, not knowing what they were, when Sylvia walked into the kitchen. Looking at me she said inquisitively, "What are you doing?"

"Sorry love," I replied, "It's not me, you have not cleared the dinner plates".

Sylvia walked up closer and peered into the bowl and exclaimed, "Oh no, you are washing up the steak for tomorrow's dinner".

We were due to have some friends around for a meal the following day and Sylvia had cut up some braising steak and left it in a saucepan as she thought, out of reach of my eager hands. Needless to say she was most upset with me and I tried to redeem the situation by suggesting that I rinsed out the steak under the cold water tap and in that way no one would ever know. You will be glad to know that she was horrified by the suggestion and our guests the following evening enjoyed a lovely steak casserole, marinated in something far more pleasurable than washing up liquid.

Luncheon club laughs

Over the years one of the things I have enjoyed doing is to be able to attend luncheon clubs and talk about some of my experiences. One such invitation took me to a very posh do at a ladies luncheon club in Stratford-upon-Avon. I was given a very warm welcome, my talk was really well received, and I travelled home feeling a great sense of satisfaction. The jokes had all gone down well as had the meal and somewhat exceptionally, I had been very well remunerated. It felt like a good day as I arrived home and relaxed in the armchair.

Within a few minutes my son Ian arrived home bright and breezy as usual. As he entered the lounge he said "Hi Dad", he then laughed a little and said, "What are you doing?"

"Sitting here relaxing," I said

"Yes but why are you sitting like that?" enquired Ian.

"Like what?" I asked in a somewhat perplexed tone.

"Dad, you haven't been to Stratford like that have you?" asked Ian.

By this time I was getting a bit impatient and said, "For goodness sake Ian what is your problem?"

"I hate to tell you Dad, but you have one black shoe and one grey shoe."

Of course once Sylvia came in and saw me she was horrified because she will often get my clothes from the wardrobe for me just to make sure they all match in terms of style and colour. On this occasion however I had done it myself hence the mistake. Sylvia always felt that this reflected badly on her and she was most upset that no one had told me that I was wearing odd shoes. For my part however I am glad I hadn't known, definitely a case I feel of ignorance being bliss.

Wallpaper woes

When Sylvia and I were first looking to buy a house in Solihull we went to view a particular property. On ringing the doorbell Mrs Jones opened the door and greeted us with a reassuring "Good morning". After the customary handshakes she began to show us around downstairs and I remember being very impressed by the size of the living room – ideal for our growing family I thought to myself. When Mrs Jones was taking us upstairs she made what I thought at the time was a strange remark.

"Oh, I just want to say that the wallpaper in the bathroom is not my choice."

We arrived at the top of the stairs, walked across the landing and looked at the three good-sized bedrooms. I was beginning to get a good feeling about this house. We then entered the bathroom and immediately I was struck by what I thought was an amazing contrast of colours.

I have said earlier that I can see light and dark and some bright colours if they are close up. Well what I saw was the light of the bath, hand basin and toilet which contrasted sharply with what looked to me like black walls. I had never seen black walls before and my natural instinct was to reach out and touch. As my fingers made contact with the wall I was impressed by the beautiful texture which was smooth and velvet like to the touch. There was also an embossed pattern on the paper and I said to Sylvia, "Wow this paper is absolutely gorgeous, such fantastic quality and what a pattern!"

At this point Sylvia nudged me in the ribs, which usually means, be quiet.

However, I continued feeling the paper and saying once again, "No it is really lovely and such a pretty embossed pattern too".

I then felt Sylvia's elbow sharper than ever in my side and I knew I had overstepped the mark.

Mrs Jones led us downstairs and as we stepped outside both Sylvia and I remarked to her that we liked the house and we would be back in touch with an offer. With the door shut behind us Sylvia laid into me.

"Sometimes John you are such an embarrassment".

"Why, what have I done?" I asked feeling a bit hurt emotionally and physically in the ribs.

"Didn't you hear the lady say that the wallpaper was not her choice" Sylvia asked.

"Yes" I replied, "but I did not know what she meant".

Sylvia responded, "What she meant was that the paper was covered with hundreds of topless women and you were feeling them all over and saying how gorgeous they were and such a lovely embossed pattern. The poor woman was going red from the neck up."

Needless to say we bought the house. The paper actually stayed on for a few years. Sylvia said I would not be corrupted by it (not more than I am already anyway!) and our daughters did actually have a great deal of fun at bath times with their pens and colouring pencils drawing clothes and moustaches on the ladies.

Two incidences eventually persuaded us to strip the paper off. Firstly Beverley had a bad dream one night that the ladies came off the wall and were chasing her and then a little while later one of the tops came off a tap in the bathroom and the water was shooting up in the air. Allison was sent to go and get Eddie, a young teacher from a couple of doors away. As Eddie was coming up the stairs Sylvia suddenly thought of our lewd wallpaper and what would our schoolteacher neighbour think about this with us being respected Churchgoers too. Sylvia felt embarrassed, apologised to Eddie as he was fixing the tap and in no time at all Sylvia had replaced the wallpaper with some more, a lot cheaper, but far less controversial, much to the disgust of some of the male visitors to our house.

Birdsong and budgerigars

Singing is a lot of fun. It brings refreshment to the one who is singing and spreads joy all around like a smile. Doctors now tell us what I learned from the Bible long ago that it is a healthy thing to have a song resonating from the heart. In my childhood I can recall that people such as the milkman or the bus driver would often be singing or whistling as they worked and as they did so it spread an aura of joy. People don't seem to do that kind of thing much today so let's start a campaign to get people singing again!

In times of hardship singing has been a great antidote to worry, it has united the people and inspired so called ordinary people to perform great feats of courage. In World War 1 one of the great hit songs was *Pack Up Your Troubles in Your Old Kit Bag and Smile*. It is a very hard thing to sing for much more than 10 minutes and stay in depression. Something happens on the inside of us as we sing a joyful song that somehow dispels the darkness around and we begin to see things from a different perspective. Again I have had to learn this secret for myself and the revelation has come through reading the bible and discovering that God is a God of song, dance, exuberant joy and a great deal of fun. I discovered that god loves me so much that he sings over me and dances around me with great excitement. He loves music because he invented music.

God also had fun in creation, especially when naming the animals. Of all of his creation I just love the birds of the air, it is a wonderful thing to wake up in the morning to the sound of the birds singing their cheerful song of joy. Many of us wake up blurry-eyed saying rather grumpily "Good Lord it's morning" instead of awaking bright-eyed and bushy-tailed with a cheery "Good morning Lord, thank you for a brand new day". Not so with the birds however, they appear to be bright and cheery everyday no matter what the weather.

Budgerigars have been pets in our family since I was a child. When I was at home with Mum and Dad nearly all budgies seemed to be called Joey and ours was no exception. Since being married we have only had three budgies. The first was yellow looking similar to a canary. We called him "Chico" and he was quite a little character. He bounced up and down to the Tamla Motown song by the Miracles *Tears of a Clown* and he used to love coming out of his cage where he would walk on the floor (a dangerous thing to do with a blind man around) and then take off for a short flight before landing on anything and everything. He particularly loved landing on the heads of people much to Sylvia's terror and it got to the stage where Sylvia could not stand to be in the room while Chico was flying around.

I remember one Saturday morning I was sitting in the armchair, concentrating very hard on reading part of my Braille bible and Chico flew on to my lap and he walked across the page I was reading. I found this quite cute and amusing, until Sylvia walked in and said "Do you know that the bird is pecking your Braille dots off the page?"

I hastily flicked Chico off as I wondered to myself how many months had he been doing that? Was this the reason why I was finding so many Bible passages hard to read? Braille was difficult enough for me to read without Chico making it even more so. Pecking dots off here and there can change a word into something completely different. Nowadays if I go out to give a Bible talk I will sometimes preface the message by saying "If this is heresy don't blame me, blame the budgie".

Children will be children

My own children of course have grown up with a blind Dad so they have in a sense never known anything different. I am sure there were times when they would have wished I had been able to see, but on the whole I think they have been okay about it and they have certainly had a lot of fun at my expense, which I think is great.

When my daughters were of infant school age they would occasionally bring one or two of the friends to the house and introduce them to me. I remember one occasion when Sara brought a friend into our house. I was sitting in the armchair (probably listening to my radio) and I had not realised that Sara was waving her hands up and down in front of my face. She then exclaimed to her friend, "You see I told you he can't see; look he's not blinking".

In recent years I decided that for my birthday I would like a photograph album with postcard size pictures of the Aston Villa players to be put into the album. Why I wanted this I do not know but just put it down to one of my eccentricities. To humour me, Sylvia made the eight mile trip into Birmingham City Centre to purchase a nice photograph album and promptly went along to the Aston Villa shop to get the photographs. She was to be disappointed, however, because they had none in stock. Being summer they were awaiting a new batch before the start of the new season. Sylvia made the journey home feeling more than a little disconsolate that my requested birthday present was not going to materialise.

Later than evening my daughter Beverley rang up from her home in the North East of England. I was out at the time and so she chatted with her Mum, who proceeded to tell her about her unsatisfactory trip to Birmingham for the photographs. Beverley expressed surprise that her Dad should want a photograph album for his birthday when he could not see the photographs and Sylvia replied by saying, "But, you know your Dad".

Then Beverley came up with what they both thought was a great idea. "Why don't you fill the album up with family photographs Mum? Dad will never know the difference if you just tell him the names of each player". Apparently they laughed and laughed at this idea, but in actual fact Sylvia could not go through with it. However, she did tell me all about the plan and I roared with laughter because I thought it was such a marvellous idea and it showed to me that Beverley had a completely healthy attitude towards me not seeing.

On my birthday Beverley did telephone to see how I was and if I had received anything nice as a present. I said, "Yes Beverley, I've had a wonderful photograph album with all of the Aston Villa players in it". I was really winding her up and I could sense some feeling of guilt and embarrassment in her voice on the other end of the phone. Eventually I could stand it no longer and I dissolved into laughter as I let Beverley know that I was aware of her fiendish idea and I thought it was absolutely great. She said that she had felt guilty afterwards, but I reassured her that it was okay and I for my part thought it was a marvellous idea.

Pink Flamingo

One Wednesday night while I was still a student in London I decided to go with two blind friends, Neville and Mike, to the Pink Flamingo club for a soul disco. The club was located in Wardour Street and we had to get there on the tube from Notting Hill Gate. We duly arrived in the vicinity of the Pink Flamingo but we were not quite sure where Wardour Street was in relation to the tube station. If you can picture the scene therefore; three young blind men walking arm in arm (so as not to all go off in different directions) all carrying white sticks.

It was not long before a gentleman enquired as to where we were going and did we need some assistance. Mike piped up saying, "Thanks mate, we are looking for Wardour Street and the Pink Flamingo".

"Fine, I'll take you there" said the man coming in between Neville and me and now making up a foursome. Good job the pavements were wide around there. Now picture the scene: four men arm in arm with three white sticks. Must have looked very interesting.

With the aid of our Good Samaritan we were striding out confidently when to our surprise a very confident sounding lady stopped us in our tracks and asked if we needed any assistance. This time it was my turn to say, "No thanks, we're heading for the Pink Flamingo".

To our astonishment she promptly wheeled us around, linked arms between Neville and the other gentleman whilst at the same time saying, "You are heading in the wrong direction, so let me take you there."

Our Good Samaritan gentleman friend was left speechless; Neville and I were nonplussed at these events whilst Mike was almost choking trying to hold back his laughter. I am sure you can picture the scene now. Four men, one woman all arm in arm and three white sticks. Anyway give the mystery lady her due, she got us safely into the Pink Flamingo having asked the doorman to "Take care of these four gentlemen would you? They're blind."

When safely inside and we were sure the woman had gone we all burst into uncontrollable fits of laughter, all except our male helper that is who was clearly embarrassed and after wishing us a pleasant evening made a hasty exit. One thing I have always wondered however, is if that woman had not come along, where would we have ended up?

Steak mistakes

Whilst still at college in London, my friend Mike, had received some particularly impressive examination results from his shorthand typing tests and as part of his celebration he invited me to go with him to one of his favourite steak houses. This was at a time when I was still very nervous about eating out, but I somewhat reluctantly agreed. It helped knowing that Mike was also blind, though much more confident and extrovert than me. We arrived at Mike's chosen restaurant and I was very much guided by him as to what we ordered from the menu. I recall that we each had a sirloin cooked rare to medium.

While we were waiting for the meals to arrive Mike decided that he needed to visit the toilet. When he returned the meals had already landed on our table, brought to us by a very efficient and well-mannered waiter. Part of my dread was having a really tough steak and not being able to cut it. However, it was incredibly tender and I managed brilliantly (even if I do say so myself) to cut the steak and savour its delicious juices, along with the chips, mushrooms, onion rings and peas. Mike and I did not converse much at this time. I was too busy facing up to the delightful challenge in front of me to talk, but I did become aware of Mike hacking away at the contents on his plate.

"Is your steak tough Mike" I enquired.

"It bloody well is, tough as old boots. What about yours?" came his animated reply.

"No, mine's absolutely fine, really succulent" I responded, still deliciously chewing away.

On hearing the sound of the waiter's voice at the next table Mike called out in a firm voice, "Excuse me, but this steak is really very tough".

The waiter quickly drew alongside our table and almost instantly began to chuckle, "Pardon me Sir" he said, "that is not your steak you are trying to cut up, but it's your tie. The steak Sir is now sitting on the table at the side of your plate."

How it happened we do not know, maybe when Mike came back from the loo he had let his tie dangle on to his plate, but whatever, we laughed so much we almost cried. Mike, however, had the last laugh because they not only brought him a fresh meal but also said he could have his steak on the house.

A quick look at the dictionary shows me that the word fun is interchangeable with pleasurable, amusing, entertaining, enjoyable and a really modern one is 'cool'. I hope that the stories listed in this section have created in you some, if not all of those emotions. We are all on a search for fun, amusement, pleasure etc. There's a good chance that if we are having fun, then others will be having fun too, even if at times it is at our expense.

I have discovered that life can be fun when we set out to give others a fun time. I loved Christmas when I was a child. Nothing could compare to the thrill of unwrapping presents on Christmas morning, or so I thought. When I became a parent and my children were old enough to enjoy Christmas, it was equally, if not more thrilling, to feel their excitement and sense of fun as they opened their presents. Now as a grandparent I am going through that all again. Yes, it can be great fun creating enjoyment for other people.

Sometimes we have to decide to have fun. We have to break out of the routine of life and start to do the fun stuff. I never used to think that way but since I invited Jesus to come and live in my heart, fun has become an integral part of my life. Let me tell you then of some of the fun stuff that I have done or become involved with.

Blackpool

I remember walking home one October night. It was about 5pm and I knew that Sylvia would have our three daughters (all under 5 years of age) in their pyjamas and ready for bed. The thought came into my head, "Wouldn't it be great to drive off to Blackpool now and let the kids see the illuminations".

I was still mulling over these outlandish thoughts when I entered the house to be greeted with hugs and kisses from the pyjama-clad children with the usual pleas "Daddy, can we have a story before we go to bed?"

"Sure," I said, "but just a few moments while I talk to mummy".

Sylvia was in the kitchen so as the girls went back to playing their make believe games I went in to speak with her. As Sylvia was putting the dirty clothes into her new washing machine (I'll tell you about that next) I blurted out "Do you fancy taking the kids to Blackpool to see the illuminations?"

Sylvia turned towards me and said, "When, on Saturday?"

"No, now" I replied.

"You must be crazy" said Sylvia in a somewhat incredulous tone.

With that I disappeared into the living room to be with the kids and to allow my wild musings about Blackpool to subside. A few minutes later Sylvia emerged from the kitchen and asked me out of earshot of the children whether I was really serious about going to Blackpool there and then. She knew I was of course, and once I had reaffirmed this, to my utter surprise she said, "Let's do it then".

With that I said to the kids, "Come on girls, we're going on an adventure". That was it, I had their attention and I remember that we left their pyjamas on, just putting trousers, socks, anoraks etc. over the top so that they would be nice and warm. Of course they were so excited and wanted to know where we were going and I said I would tell them in the car.

Within 15 minutes we were out of the house, cruising along in our recently acquired blue Ford Escort (I'll tell you about that shortly too). It was about 6.30pm as we headed off towards Spaghetti Junction to take the M6 North bound. Soon into the journey and with three excited little girls in the back of the car, I proceeded to tell them a story of someone's great night out to see the pretty lights in a place called Blackpool. I then let the cat out of the bag to indicate that that was where we were going on our adventure. None of us will ever forget the events of that night, it was truly magical for all of us.

We arrived in Blackpool after a trouble free trip at about 9pm stayed there for two to three hours going the full length of the Golden Mile as well as visiting the famous Pleasure Beach for a whole host of rides and then set off home with three tired but very happy children in the back. Sylvia did a great job with the driving and thankfully it was only me who had to be up early in the morning.

New house

Houses and cars have formed an amazing part of our life as a family and much of it will be revealed in this book, but for now I will restrict the saga so as to illustrate the fun aspect. At the age of 25 I had never actually lived in a house with a garden and I longed for that. I would imagine sitting out in the summer listening to the cricket on my radio and it sounded idyllic, but would it ever happen to me I wondered. We were living in an upstairs three bedroom council maisonette at the time, where in fact all of our three girls had been born. Someone told us that a three-bedroom house had become empty just around the corner in Lakes Road. Wyrley Birch Estate in the Erdington area of Birmingham. Sylvia and I could not resist going to have a look at the house, peering in through the front windows at the long living room and even lifting the letterbox to look into the hall and up the stairs. It looked good to us, ideal for our growing family and wonder of wonders, it even had a small back garden.

I became very proactive at this point and immediately went home and telephoned the Council Housing office and requested an interview, which I was able to obtain for the next day. I duly arrived at the office in good time for the interview and was seen by a most understanding lady who listened sympathetically as I explained our housing need, indicating along the way just how perfect the particular house in Lakes Road would be for us. The housing officer listened to my request very sympathetically and asked appropriate questions. She told me that I had put forward a very convincing case but warned there was very stiff competition for such properties. She went on to say that I should hear something within the week. I left feeling quietly confident.

In the days that followed we prayed a lot about that house and we were overjoyed when the postman arrived with a letter from the Birmingham Housing Department stating that we were being offered the very house we had requested in Lakes Road. This sure felt like fun and within a few days we were moving in to my very first house with a garden. After we had been in for a week or two, Sylvia and I felt that we would like a house-warming party with a difference. We felt so profoundly grateful to God for blessing us with this gift so we planned a night of thanksgiving to God plus one of Sylvia's exceptional buffet-type meals.

We sent out invitations to friends far and wide, explaining why we wanted them to join in this celebration with us. About 30 people gathered in our living room on that momentous night for an evening of singing praise to God, prayers of thanksgiving and to dedicate the house to God's service. One or two people brought presents even though we had stipulated that no presents were required but the biggest surprises were saved for later in the night when all the people had gone home. As we began to tidy up we started to find money scattered around hidden behind cushions, at the back of the clock on the mantelpiece, on the stereo, in the kitchen and so on. There were £5, £10 and £20 notes and even a cheque for £50. Later when we went up to bed we even found money in the bed and later in the week discovered money in the biscuit tin. It was truly an amazing evening and whoever it was who came up with the idea of leaving all that money around certainly made it a whole lot of fun for us.

Ask and you shall receive!

During the course of the house-warming evening Sylvia had an unusual conversation with a friend of ours in the kitchen. The friend in question, Jenny, was keen to know how Sylvia managed without an automatic washing machine. At the time we just had an old fashioned electric boiler which was supplied by the Council and already installed when we moved into the house. This was in the days before disposable nappies so with the twins still only being a few months old there was a lot of washing to be done.

Jenny, having compassion for Sylvia and wanting to see some of her time freed up, said "Why don't you pray and ask God for an automatic washing machine?"

I think Sylvia was stunned by such a question, it not entering her head to even imagine such a thing would be possible. After that we did discuss the idea and though we certainly could not afford such a luxury, I do believe that the seed had been sewn in Sylvia's heart and from time to time she did mention the matter to God in prayer, obviously not seriously expecting much, in light of what was to happen next.

Sylvia was home with the children one morning when the doorbell rang. When she got to the door a deliveryman thrust a piece of paper at her and said "Can you sign for this please madam?"

Sylvia inquisitively asked, "What is it I'm signing for?" as she noticed a huge box being wheeled down the path by the man's colleague.

"I don't know madam, I'm just paid to deliver the goods" said the man.

"But I haven't bought anything" insisted Sylvia.

By now the deliveryman was getting a bit frustrated and said "That's not my problem. Can I wheel this inside and get on my way?"

The big box safely inside, the two men left and went about their business. When I arrived home an hour or two later Sylvia was still mystified and she had been wondering whether I had ordered something without telling her or was this delivered to us by mistake?

I was excited and keen to open our mystery box. I eventually persuaded my dear wife that it would be good to open it, if only to see what it was. With eager anticipation we tore off the metal fasteners and began to slit the tape that was around the lid of this massive cardboard box. Once inside we lifted out the packing to gradually discover a front-loading automatic washing machine. There was a short note taped to the top of the machine which read "A Gift from the Lord – Fully Paid – Psalm 34 Verse 10, which I now know says "The young lions lack and go hungry, but those who trust in the Lord lack no good thing".

Sylvia's reaction was to burst into tears saying, "I can't believe it".

We moved the appliance to the kitchen where it stayed for about a week, still primarily in its unwrapped state. About a week later we received a phone call from a certain friend named Jenny, yes that's right, the one who said that Sylvia should pray for a washing machine. This time on the phone she asked Sylvia if anything interesting had happened. At first Sylvia, playing Jenny up, said "No nothing at all" but after a moment or two said "Yes! As a matter of fact it has. We have had this huge package and we do not know where it has come from".

"Oh that's good" said a relieved sounding Jenny, "it's not from us but the people who it is from want to remain anonymous and for you to give the glory to God, for it was He who put it on their heart".

"But I haven't got a clue what to do with it" said a concerned Sylvia

"You must not worry about that" affirmed Jenny, "a plumber friend of ours will be over in the next few days to plumb it in and set it all up for you".

The machine achieved what it was sent for in that it was a great blessing to Sylvia, lasting many years and freeing up a considerable amount of precious time for her.

Ford Escort

When we lived in the first floor maisonette, after the unexpected arrival of twins, it meant initially that we had three children all under one year old. I was out working all day at the Inland Revenue and life became very difficult for Sylvia in the day. Getting three little children ready to go out was a big job in itself, let alone getting them down four flights of stairs in a twin pushchair (no lift) and then back up again on their return. It was almost impossible for Sylvia to get out and about, though my Mum, who lived nearby was always willing to lend a hand wherever possible.

Needless to say I felt some responsibility for the predicament my wife was in and as I became more and more aware of the physical demands being made on her I found myself searching my own heart as to what could be done to relieve her of some of the burden. I was already well into my practice of getting up early in the morning to pray before going to work and on this one particular morning I felt a heavy burden to pray for Sylvia. I remember throwing myself on to my knees, burying my head in the armchair and crying to God in desperation for help. I felt deeply concerned for my lovely wife and I needed God to hear my cry on her behalf.

As I poured my heart out to him I had this very strong impression come into my heart, almost as a phrase, "Sylvia needs to learn to drive". I could not get this thought out of my mind and so I gave up trying to pray and went off to work feeling a little disconsolate.

Next morning exactly the same pattern emerged and the morning after that and the morning after that and so on. Eventually I began to suspect that this wacky thought might just be from God. Not quite on the building an ark in the desert proportions, but not far off in my view. We could hardly make ends meet financially anyway, so how could we afford driving lessons, let alone buy and run a car.

By this time I was just beginning to discover that God was a God of fun and of doing the seemingly impossible but I was still very much a novice in these areas. However, God had convinced me, now we had to convince Sylvia. I needed to broach the subject carefully and choose my moment with great skill, but even then I knew it would not be easy. When I did seize my opportunity my worst fears were realised.

"My love, I think God is saying you should take driving lessons" I said nervously.

Sylvia gave a derisory laugh and said "Oh yes, in my spare time! That is just about the craziest idea you've ever come out with".

"Yes I know, but I am convinced it is God's idea and He will provide" I replied, much more confidently this time.

Sylvia could see I was serious and to her eternal credit she agreed that if it was really God's idea then she would go along with it. We knew someone through church who was a driving instructor and after speaking with him he agreed to give Sylvia driving lessons at half the regular price. Another sign I thought that God was in this.

After the first few driving lessons Sylvia would come home shaking with fear. Denis, her driving instructor was heard to say, "She'll be a hard nut to crack, but we'll get there". In the end Sylvia took her driving test and she passed her test first time and when she rang to tell me the news I was so proud of her.

While Sylvia was still in the process of taking driving lessons, something remarkable happened one Saturday. It was fairly early in the morning and we were just sitting down for breakfast when there was a knock on the door. I went to answer it and was greeted by a cheerful sounding man with more than a hint of a London accent.

"Hi John, it's Chris Thacker, here from Croydon – you remember you visited our church a few months back".

Chris and his wife Janet were youth leaders at Woodside Baptist Church in Croydon and as he had rightly said I had been there to speak only a short while before. Now he was on my doorstep with his wife saying that they had just dropped off for breakfast en route to their holidays in the Peak District of Derbyshire.

What seemed strange to us was that Chris and Janet were in no hurry to get away after breakfast. In fact they were still with us for dinner and for tea. We chatted about lots of things, mainly to do with family and church issues. After tea Chris got his car keys out of his pocket and I thought that this was the indication that they were about to leave and indeed they were, but not before Chris had lobbed the keys across the room and landed them right into Sylvia's lap.

"What are these?" asked my startled wife.

"They're the keys to your car" said Chris calmly.

"But I don't have a car" said Sylvia with Janet and me looking on intently.

"You do now" Chris responded, "The Lord has told us that we are to give you Janet's Escort. Would you like to take a look at it?"

This was truly an awesome moment for us. Our children soundly asleep in their cots totally unaware that their Mum had just become the proud owner of a beautiful Ford Escort that was only 18 months old with just 11,000 miles on the clock. Chris and Janet took a totally bewildered Sylvia for a little test drive before leaving in their other car to commence their holiday in the knowledge that they had been obedient in doing what God had asked them to do.

I know that they had fun in giving their car away, even more so when they arrived home from holiday to find that their house sale had gone through and the house they wanted to buy had been dropped in price by several thousand pounds during the week they were away. God truly rewarded them for their generosity and obedience to his voice.

For our part, we had some great times of fun in that car not just in spontaneous trips like the one to Blackpool but also in the day to day help it afforded Sylvia in simply getting out and about to the shops, local parks and to visit family and friends. God had surely heard my desperate cry and answered in spectacular fashion.

Marriage fun

Whilst not always succeeding of course, I have made it a practice to try and inject barrel loads of fun into my marriage with Sylvia. We have passed through many trials and dark valleys during our 36 years together, however, we have managed to laugh our way through many of them and come out the other side much stronger individually and with a deeper love for each other.

Believe it or not, God has that same desire for you and me and as a married man I believe that can all come within my existing relationship. I am committed to having a wild, passionate affair with my wife. Someone has said that any man can go from woman to woman having sex, but it takes a really great lover to keep one woman fulfilled and happy for a lifetime. With the inspiration of God my creator living in me, I want to be the very best lover I can be and that means satisfying the very deepest needs of my wife in all areas, not just the bedroom.

Here are some of the things that I try to do in order to keep the fun, fire, passion and excitement in our marriage.

- Be up early in the morning to pray, especially for my wife and so set the atmosphere for the day. She is my lover and apart from God, she takes first place in my life.
- Make a point of telling her that I love her at least once a day and show affection every day with a hug, or a touch and a little flirting. We did it before we were married and it felt good, so why stop now?
- Regularly show appreciation for the work she does in keeping a nice home, doing the washing, the cooking and a myriad of other things.
- Remember birthdays, Mother's Day and most of all our Wedding Anniversary. These are all wonderful opportunities to make my wife feel really extra special.

In a busy life, plan days or nights together. Block everything else out of your diary for that day or night and say "That time is for my wife". Then take a drive into the country and/or have an evening in to watch a movie and share cheese and wine together. Keep the telephone switched off and ignore the doorbell (unless it's an emergency!) Do something spontaneous occasionally, like book a few days away at a hotel or get tickets for a show. When you get hurt or offended, which you will because we are human, forgive quickly and respond with an act of kindness to bless your partner to prevent bitterness setting in.

In essence I believe that whilst fun can be spontaneous, in a marriage it often requires planning, imagination and effort. That said if we apply ourselves to do some of these things then the rewards can be tremendous, and the only affair that we need ever consider is a passionate one with our life partner. This little acronym will show you the ingredients required in any ongoing passionate relationship.

A Appreciation

F Fun

F Forgiveness

A Affection

I Intimacy

R Romance

Section Three – FAITH

The dictionary tells me that faith means assurance, confidence, conviction, reliance and trust. It certainly embodies all of those things and much more besides. I have come to regard faith as one of my most favourite words in the world, vying for supremacy alongside such greats as love and forgiveness.

There are many kinds of faith of course. Every time we walk into a room and sit on a chair we exercise faith in that chair to take our weight don't we? That is unless you are in the habit of testing out the chair beforehand of course and I have never met anyone who does that.

We put our faith in people very often and then get extremely hurt or disappointed when they fail to live up to our expectations. We put our faith in machines to do the things they were made to do and so we could go on.

The faith I want to tell you about however is the faith that totally transformed my life and turned me from being a person who was full of fear and timidity to one who is now able to live a life free from fear and over many years now has been able to undertake exploits of faith.

The great exchange

It was the beginning of May 1968. I was in the audio typing classroom at Pembridge Place along with three other students, Ian, Barbara and Chris. We were just building up to our RSA Audio Typing (Elementary and Intermediate Level) exams. Towards the end of the lesson our teacher, Mrs Craig, said, "I think you all know that my husband and I attend Church each week and we were wondering if you would like to come along with us some time?"

There was an embarrassed silence for a moment or two before Mrs Craig broke that silence by saying, "You're a Christian aren't you John?"

I felt awkward at this question being directed at me and muttered back hesitantly, "Yes, I think I am".

"You don't sound too sure about it" came our teacher's reply, "maybe we can talk about it sometime".

Later on that evening as I lay on my bed after tea Mrs Craig's question was still bothering me. Was I a Christian or not and did it really matter? My thoughts were interrupted as Graham, one of the three lads I shared a room with came in to talk about cricket, before I set off back to the classroom because we always had work set for us in the evening by our diligent, hard-working teacher. I was not prepared however for the long night that lay ahead as I tossed and turned in my bed all night bombarded by questions in my mind, all triggered off by Mrs Craig's question as to whether I was a Christian or not.

I know that my turning back and forth on my squeaky mattress disturbed my room-mates, but I could not help it. I was going through mental and emotional turmoil. One question after another kept on rising up and assailing my mind. Thoughts like, am I a Christian? Does it really matter whether I am or not? Is there a Heaven and is there a Hell? And where will I go when I die left me in turmoil for much of the night. From that night on I did think about those questions quite a lot, but never coming up with any suitable answers.

On the evening of 29th May a crowd of us gathered in the lounge at Pembridge because the European Cup Final at Wembley Stadium between Manchester United and Portuguese champions Benfica, whose side included the great Eusebio, was being shown on BBC television. It was a great final which Manchester United won in impressive style, but it was actually during half time that I experienced a conversation that led to a watershed moment in my life.

Most of the lads nipped off to the kitchen for refreshments, but I stayed behind to listen to the half time summary. On that night our teacher Mrs Craig was on staff duty and she just happened to wonder into the lounge during half time in the game. She quietly drew alongside me and said quietly, "Did you think any more about my question John?"

Knowing full well what she meant, I asked, "Which question was that?"

"The one about whether or not you are a Christian" Mrs Craig replied.

I then told Mrs Craig about my troubled night on the evening that she had asked the question and I explained that I had always thought I was a Christian, regularly saying the Lord's Prayer before going to sleep at night. She concluded by saying that she felt that God was speaking to me and that we should talk further at another time, but thankfully she was sensitive and left the room in good time for what turned out to be a very exciting conclusion to the big match.

Over the course of the next few weeks I did think about religion a lot, turning all kinds of questions around in my mind. Mrs Craig did talk briefly with me on one further occasion, but she felt that it would really benefit me if I could meet with a couple of friends of hers, who had previously been at Pembridge and were now attending Westminster Chapel.

The mystery couple were named Tony and Margaret Abbot and as it turned out they rang and invited me to join them for tea at their flat in Acton. I agreed and duly made my way up there by tube. It turned out to be a very pleasant, introductory type of an evening where religion was just one of many topics we covered in conversation. Both Tony, a softly spoken, rugby loving Welshman and Margaret, a cheerful Irish lass, were registered blind. Tony, an architect by profession, had been blinded as the result of a motor cycle accident whereas Margaret had lost her sight due to the effects of diabetes.

I was to meet Tony and Margaret again on a few occasions briefly over the course of the next few months, but it was into September of that year before I was to spend a life-changing weekend with them. By that time I had finished my typing course at Pembridge, having gained distinctions in my audio typing exams and was in the process of applying for the previously mentioned job at the Ministry of Overseas Development in Clerkenwell. Tony had rung my parents' home in Birmingham and issued an invitation for me to go and spend a weekend with them in Acton. Tony and Margaret were at Victoria Coach Station to meet me and in no time at all we were back at their little ground floor flat in Acton where we enjoyed a pleasant buffet supper together. After some general conversation and a bit more of a getting to know you session we retired to bed ready for the more important matters that were to follow on Saturday and Sunday.

Next morning after breakfast Margaret went off shopping leaving Tony and me to chat. Having said that, it was mainly Tony who did the talking explaining how it was that he had become involved with Christianity. In no time at all Margaret was back from the shops and once she had put her stuff away she came in and joined in with the conversation. Tony filled his wife in with what we had been talking about and then it was her turn to explain to me how she had become a Christian and of the difference it had made to her life.

In turn I explained that I had been christened as a baby and I was of the opinion that that made me a Christian. Tony pointed out that you would not find that in the Bible. He told me that Jesus's response to a devout religious man called Nicodemus who asked "What must I do to have eternal life?" was "You must be born again".

We discussed matters well into the afternoon and early evening, only pausing at around 5 o'clock to listen to Sports Report on BBC radio so that we could catch up on all of the football results. As we sat down for our evening meal, the highlight of which was, a very tasty mixed grill, there was, what was to me, a very unusual record playing in the background. I quickly recognised the voice as that of Cliff Richard, known to me then only for his pop music and film career. On this record, however, Cliff was singing traditional hymns such as *What A Friend We Have In Jesus* and *When I Survey The Wondrous Cross* along with Gospel favourites such as *It Is No Secret What God Can Do* and *Take My Hand Precious Lord*. It was certainly very nice to listen to and Margaret explained that this was Cliff's first gospel album as he had only become a Christian about one year before.

Before going off to bed that night my charming hosts asked if I would like to go to Church with them the following morning or evening. I said that I would give it some thought but my opinion was that I would probably sit it out. I think I slept well that night, despite all the things going round my brain; I was probably exhausted with it all.

Next morning following a breakfast of cereals, boiled egg and toast, Tony and Margaret got themselves ready for Church and I kept to my word and stayed at home. They left me with a wide choice of music to play while they were away and I also had with me my ever present pocket radio. In that quiet couple of hours I had plenty of time to reflect and wondered why it was that I had been so uptight about going to Church. "I may have found some answers" I mused to myself, and I considered whether I should go with Tony and Margaret to the 6.30pm evening service. That would really thrill them I thought.

By the time they arrived home, the roast lamb smelt delicious in the oven. That was a special treat for me because Margaret had asked me what my favourite roast dinner was. I had realised by this time that Margaret's lack of sight did not impair her ability in the kitchen in the slightest way for she was an excellent cook. Tony said that they had had a good time at Church and in turn I said that I had enjoyed playing some of their records, having particularly enjoyed listening most attentively to Cliff's Gospel album called *Good News*. I then broke the news that they were eagerly awaiting by saying that I would go to Church with them on the night. They tried hard to contain their excitement, but I know they were delighted.

It seemed no time at all before we were on the tube heading up to Westminster Chapel. I was extremely nervous as we approached the Church. As we stepped inside I remember being surprised at how big the Church building seemed and how many people were attending. It also sounded from the voices that there were a lot of younger people there, which again was a bit of a shock to me because I was under the impression that it was mainly old people who went to Church. I've heard it said that you never get a second chance to make a first impression and in this case my impression was of a warm, friendly group of people of all ages and it did not feel religious in the way that I had expected.

We quickly found our way to a pew, shook hands with a few people and then it was time for the start of the service. I cannot remember what we sang, but I do remember that it was wholehearted and pretty uplifting. Surprisingly, however, I do remember the sermon, that was the part I thought I would fall asleep at, but in truth it was a very interesting and challenging message, very well delivered by the preacher. He spoke from the book of Ruth in the Old Testament of the bible, a book which I did not know existed before then. It is a very short book, but it is a beautiful love story between Ruth and a man called Boaz. I have always been a sucker for a good love story and this one had me well and truly hooked. The preacher spoke a lot about God's love and drew examples from the life of Boaz.

He also introduced the subject of sin and every time he mentioned that word, although I felt uncomfortable, I thought he was talking about other people in the congregation. Perhaps there were some real sinners present like bank robbers or rapists etc. I certainly did not regard myself as a sinner. In fact I was in the process of justifying myself by thinking of all the kind acts I had done or would do if the circumstances were right, when the preacher metaphorically hit me right between the eyes. He quoted a verse from the Bible saying "All your good deeds are like filthy rags to a Holy God". I immediately felt incensed, thinking, "What a cheek! Who does he think he is to talk about people like that?"

At the end of the service I felt that I still had many unresolved questions. I knew that Tony and Margaret wanted to stay behind for an hour or so for coffee and a chat, but part of me wanted to make a quick getaway. While I was still making up my mind, however, I was introduced to a young man called Mark, who helped lead a young people's Bible study and fellowship group at the Church called Antioch. Mark shook my hand firmly and asked how I had enjoyed the service. I said that I had enjoyed it very much and that there were lots of questions still buzzing around in my head. "Such as what?" he enquired

I thought for a moment and said "Can you prove to me that Jesus was actually raised from the dead and that he is alive today?"

Mark then gave me what was one of the most disappointing answers of all time followed quickly by a pearl of wisdom. He said, "I cannot prove it, nor can anyone else, but then neither can I prove to you that I love my wife. If, however, you were to come and live in our house for a month, I would hope that you would then come to the conclusion that I do love my wife. In other words you would have experienced the love that is present in our home. In the same way, if by faith you believe that Jesus died for your sins upon the Cross and you then invite Him to come and live in your heart as your Lord and Saviour, in about a month's time you will know that He is alive because you will have experienced Him and felt Him moving in your life".

What a brilliant answer that was for it seemed to dispel the vast majority of my questions. I was still struggling however with the questions of me being a sinner and why did Jesus have to die. By now we were in a side room with what sounded like about 40 people and a friend of Tony's had already brought me a cup of coffee and a biscuit. I sat there quietly by myself for several minutes and in that time it was almost as if I had pulled a one arm bandit and the lemons came down one by one and lined themselves up and things seemed to fall into place as far as my questions about eternity were concerned.

Almost instantly I knew that I was a sinner and that Jesus had come from heaven to pay the price for my sins in His own body upon the Cross. Because He is God He rose from the dead and after 40 days on Earth during which He appeared to many groups of people He ascended into heaven from where He now has all rule and authority. In that sovereign moment I received Jesus as my Lord and Saviour.

As I came to the end of my cup of coffee I was heard to say "I've got it!"

The person sitting next to me said "Did you say something?"

"Oh yes" I replied, "I've seen it, I believe in Jesus".

In no time at all I was surrounded by Tony and Margaret, together with Mark and several other people, hugging me and shaking hands reassuring me that this would be the greatest decision I could ever make. In fact just to make sure I was truly as they say 'Born Again', Mark insisted on saying a little prayer with me that I repeated line by line after him, which went along these lines:

"Dear God, I want to thank you for loving me so much that you allowed your only son Jesus Christ to come and die for me. Thank you that my sins are forgiven. I now receive Jesus as my Lord and Saviour. I thank you that I am now forgiven and that I have the free gift of everlasting life. Amen."

Everybody was so happy for me, but I did not feel any different. Obviously Tony and Margaret were overjoyed, as would Mrs Craig be when they told her. I left for home that weekend with the encouragement ringing in my ears to talk to Jesus every day, find a good Church and to read the Bible verses that had been brailed out for me by Tony.

In the ensuing weeks I told many people about my 'born again' experience and almost without exception I was laughed to scorn. My Mum and Dad were very upset because they had taken the decision to have me christened as a baby and now as an adult it seemed as if I was pouring cold water on that practice. (Pun intended!) I did feel inwardly that something wonderful had happened to me at Westminster Chapel, but bombarded with all of this negativity and ridicule caused me to have many doubts leading up to that point on the London to Birmingham coach, when I cried out to God for a girlfriend and he answered me spectacularly with the provision of Sylvia!

This was it then, the great exchange had taken place. I had swapped all of my fears for the faith that God gives. I had begun my walk of faith and I want in the succeeding pages to relive some of the experiences that I have gone through in the hope that what I have to share will help you to find faith for yourself.

I have discovered that faith is like a muscle and the more you exercise it the more it grows and the stronger it gets. At the time of writing I have now had nearly 37 years of learning to live and walk by faith so I would hope to have at the very least, a few helpful things to pass on. I trust you will stay with me for the journey.

Being born again

The term 'born again' is used to describe someone who has invited Jesus into their heart and made a declaration to follow him. The term is most apt because, as I discovered, you are starting a brand new life. You are like a new born baby in that you don't quite know where to start when it comes to prayer, reading the Bible, finding the right church etc. I had my few Bible verses brailed out that were given to me by Tony and I read them over and over again. That was probably very good for me because it ensured I remembered the truths they contained and also that I did not get spiritual indigestion from trying to take in too much. These are the Bible verses I was given:

For God so loved the world that He gave his only begotten Son so that whoever believes in Him will not perish but have everlasting life. (John 3:16)

If we confess our sins God is faithful and just to forgive us our sins and to cleanse us from all unrighteousness. (1 John 1:9)

He who has the Son of God has life and he who does not have the Son does not have life. (1 John 5:12)

I write these things in order that you may know that you have eternal life. (1 John 5:13)

I can do all things through Christ who gives me strength. (Philippians 4:13)

I now know that God's word (The Bible) is likened to milk for a new born baby as it gives and sustains life, but prayer was another matter. I had learned the Lord's Prayer at school but apart from that I did not know what or how to pray. However, having been encouraged by the prayer on the coach "Oh Lord please bless me with a girlfriend" I deduced that God must like that kind of heartfelt prayer.

After Sylvia and I were married we used to pray silently. For instance when we got into bed at night we would turn our backs on each other, pray our silent prayers and then as a sign that we had finished praying we would turn back to face each other. It was a couple of years before we developed the confidence to be able to pray out loud, firstly in front of each other and then in the company of others.

Finding the right church to attend posed quite a challenge in itself. Totally naive in such matters, we knew we were born Church of England so we quite logically I thought, started to attend the local Church where we were to be married. This was at St Margaret's located at Somerset Road in the Erdington area of Birmingham. The Vicar there, Reverend Power was very friendly and as indicated earlier, an Aston Villa supporter too, so that counted in his favour.

However, nice though the Vicar was, I have to say the services themselves were disappointing to me. I was looking for something of the atmosphere that I had felt at Westminster Chapel a few months earlier but at St Margaret's with its congregation of about 20, mainly elderly people it was singularly lacking in atmosphere. After a few weeks we decided to look elsewhere, but where?

I then had what might be termed, a 'brainwave'. I said to Sylvia "Maybe the biggest Church is the best". At that stage I had no idea of all of the other Christian denominational churches such as Methodist, Baptist, United Reform, Pentecostal etc., and so the good old C of E was our only option. Like any good brummie kid I knew of St Martin's in the Bull Ring and so we decided to go there.

Sylvia, at this stage, had not had a conversion experience like me, but it was not far away. We started to attend the 11am morning service and also the evening one at 6.30pm. Both services were very well attended with over 500 people at each service. The great organ sounded majestic as it pumped out the hymn tunes and I was surprised just how many hymns I knew from schooldays. It was really good to stand beside my girlfriend and later my wife and hear her singing heartily. Sylvia has a good, tuneful voice and so I know where our kids get it from. The Rector at St Martin's in those days was Canon Bryan Green, a well-known and sometimes controversial speaker throughout the 50's and 60's. When he came into the pulpit he would always begin with the same prayer "Lord uphold me that I may uplift thee". Canon Green was always interesting and challenging to listen to, but never more so than one night after he had returned from preaching in the United States of America.

On arriving at St Martin's that Sunday evening in January of 1970 there were actually song sheets in the pews along with the traditional hymn books. Sylvia read down the song sheet to find such gems as *Were You There when They Crucified My Lord, Go Tell It On The Mountain* and *Give Me Oil in My Lamp*. Definitely not the usual type of songs we would sing at St Martins. From the moment Bryan Green stood in the pulpit that night you could tell he was fired up. At one point he got us to sing *Amazing Grace* and part way through he stopped the congregation and said "If you don't sing it with more conviction and fervour you may as well go home".

Whether anybody did I don't know, but I loved it. I still do in fact whenever a preacher brings his congregation up with a jolt and lifts them out of the comfort zone, somehow it brings a fresh touch of reality to what is going on. On this occasion Bryan Green certainly did and we proceeded to sing *Amazing Grace* with the desire passion instead of going through the religious motions. That night the Rector was to introduce a new hymn that was to become one of my all-time favourites. He had heard it on his American trip and brought it back for us to enjoy and in fact his sermon that night was based on it. The hymn in question is called *I'm Not Ashamed to Own My Lord* and it has the rousing chorus *'At the Cross, at the Cross, where I first saw the light and the burden of my heart rolled away. It was there by faith I received my sight and now I am happy all the day'.*

Bryan Green had one more surprise in store that night too. At the end of his preaching he made a Billy Graham style appeal, inviting people to the front who wanted to commit their lives to Jesus. At the time we had been attending that Church for a good eight or nine months and nothing like that had ever happened before – surprising what a trip to America can do for a weary Vicar! As the congregation sang *When I Survey the Wondrous Cross*, Bryan Green continued to invite people to go forward and quietly Sylvia said to me, "I'm going forward" and in a flash she was gone. As we sang the last two lines of the hymn *Love so amazing so divine, demands my soul, my life, my all*, the tears streamed down my face because I knew that Sylvia was taking the most important step that any human being can take this side of the grave.

When Sylvia returned to join me in the pew she told me that she had received prayer from one of the Clergy by the name of Chris Mayfield, who years later became a Bishop. So now we were both, as they say, born again, and it sure felt good to be together in spirit as well as body and soul.

New job, new friends, new life!

In March 1969 I began to work as an audio typist for the Inland Revenue. Apart from the first week I was based at King Edward House in New Street in Birmingham's busy city centre. It was an area I knew well, the third floor office being situated just a few metres away from the Odeon where I had gone to see The Young Ones and queued for several James Bond movies a few years before. I worked in that office as part of a team of four typists for nearly five years and had a wonderful time. Two of my favourite characters, out of many in fact because I find all people fascinating to some degree, were Gillian and Kay. Gillian was a kind soul who performed in a local operatic society and she would often tackle her frustrations when it came to listening to inaudible dictation by bursting into song. I found that very amusing. Kay on the other hand was a different kettle of fish. She was in her late 20s, Welsh and with a fiery temper. Her way of dealing with the poor dictation was to slowly simmer until she got to boiling point and then she would ring the Tax Inspector and demand they come and listen for themselves.

I will never forget this one day when she summoned Bill Thomson to the typing room. Bill, or Mr Thomson as it was in those more austere days, was an amiable man but with a very broad Scottish accent. He did himself, or the typists no favours by mumbling into his microphone thus making him very difficult to listen to. He dutifully arrived in the typing office, cheerful as usual, to listen to his own 'dulcet' tones. He listened several times to the incoherent text and having not been able to make sense of it himself then made up something that Kay could type in. As Mr Thomson walked away he muttered something in jest about Welsh women, which totally enraged Kay and she pulled off one of her shoes and through it at the startled Inspector, who just about managed to get out of the door before the flying missile thudded into the wall, just missing his head. There was stunned silence in the room for a moment, which was then broken as Kay erupted into fits of laughter, her pent up frustration now fully released. Within a few moments she got up from her seat and went off to offer her apologies to Bill, who thankfully, not for the only time, took it all in good part.

It was Kay in fact who got me into my love of crosswords. In those days, unlike today, we actually had a scheduled 15 minute tea break, morning and afternoon. Kay or one of the other girls in the office would at about 9.30am ring down to the Hasty Tasty snack bar on the ground floor just next door to King Edward House to order the toast. My job was to nip down at 9.45 to pick up and pay for the toast.

When I arrived back a couple of minutes later, the tea would be ready and the Sun newspaper opened so that we could as a team attempt the coffee time crossword. That was fun and I really enjoyed that. It was whilst working in that office that I was to meet someone who was to become one of a group of really good friends and mentors to me as a young Christian.

As I have said in those days everything was much more formal. Rank counted for a lot and senior people were always addressed by the title of Mr, Mrs or Miss. One of the tax inspectors I used to work for was a Mr Pullinger. One morning he brought me a tape for typing and he stood by my desk for an introductory chat. After he had left the room I just happened to say to Mrs Doig, one of the more senior typists in age terms that is, "He seems like a really friendly bloke".

"Yes he is" came Mrs Doig's reply, "but just be careful because he's quite religious".

I didn't say anything at that point but a little excitement leapt on the inside of me. I thought to myself "Oh good another one, maybe he is a Christian like me". This was at the time when I was getting a lot of flak from my family and friends about being a 'born again' Christian and I was becoming desperate for some encouragement.

At lunchtime when the part time staff had gone home and the other two typists had gone for their break, I decided to give this Mr Pullinger a ring on his office extension.

"Hello Mr Pullinger" I said nervously, "this is John here from the typing office". I think he thought I was calling about his tape.

"Hello John" he said in a warm, friendly manner, "what can I do for you?"

"One of the ladies here says you're religious, so does that mean you are a Christian?"

He said that he was and I quickly told him a little of my story from Westminster Chapel, but since coming back to Birmingham I had worried my family and received criticism from friends. With that Mr Pullinger spoke some reassuring words and said that on the following day he was going to a lunchtime service at St Philip's Cathedral in Birmingham. It was a special service for half an hour geared towards business people working in the City Centre. Mr Pullinger offered to meet me at my office at 1pm and get me back for 2pm, I readily agreed and there began a long-standing friendship.

Bryan (no longer Mr Pullinger to me!) spent a lot of time with me over the next few years helping me to understand more about the Christian life that I had committed myself to. It was his wife Jenny who later suggested to Sylvia that she pray about an automatic washing machine which I wrote about earlier in the book. Bryan eventually gave up work as a tax inspector to work full time as a Pastor with Solihull Christian Fellowship.

It was through Bryan and that weekly lunchtime 30 minute service at St Philip's Cathedral that I met a group of mature Christian men who were to have a profound effect upon my life. They really helped me to establish some firm foundations of faith in my heart. For now let me tell you about three such men in particular.

Reverend David Machines was at the time on the staff of the Cathedral (Chief Diocesan Missioner, I think) and he undertook most of the Tuesday talks at the Cathedral. After a hymn and a prayer, David would teach on some theme or other for just over 20 minutes as part of a four or five week series. I found him to be a riveting speaker with loads of valuable spiritual insights with no end of interesting and amusing anecdotes. After a final prayer there was time for a cup of tea and a high quality sandwich at a very reasonable price. During this time of about 10 minutes I was able to chat with a few people before heading back with Bryan to the office. I grew to deeply love and appreciate the man and the ministry that is David MacInnes.

It was through those times at the Cathedral that I met two other people who were to play a significant part in the development of my faith. Firstly John Tupper, who was employed at the then Midland Bank in New Street. We had some good chats together and at his suggestion we would meet one lunchtime each week for coffee and sandwiches.

John lived in Sutton Coldfield with his wife Thelma and their three children. Once a month they would hold a prayer meeting in their home because they supported an organisation called Operation Mobilisation. Sylvia and I started to attend these prayer meetings at John's invitation. We would go to their house straight from work and join them for their evening meal. The prayer meetings would start at 7.30pm. We learned a lot about Operation Mobilisation and of its work around the world to spread the Christian message. We were particularly inspired by George Verwer, the founder of the movement and of the story of the two ships they had purchased to carry Bibles and other Christian literature to remote parts of the world.

At the prayer meetings Sylvia and I were becoming a little uncomfortable because everybody else prayed out audibly whereas we just prayed quietly under our breath. We both wanted to pray out loud but could not summon up the courage. We chatted with John and Thelma about our concerns and they encouraged us just to pray out something very simple like "Lord Jesus thank you for coming into my heart and for bringing me here tonight". They stressed that we did not have to pray long prayers. It was a really hard thing to pray out in public like that for the first time and it probably took us about seven or eight weeks to be able to do so. Once we had however it was such a relief and we found that we were more able to contribute to the prayer meeting after that.

The other person who became a big influence on my life was a real gentleman by the name of Maxwell Doig (no relation to the typist by the name of Mrs Doig that I mentioned earlier). Maxwell was a Senior Tax Inspector and on Wednesday lunchtimes he would hold a Bible study/prayer group in his office from 1.10pm until 1.55pm. Somewhere between 10 and 15 people would gather each week with different ones taking it in turn to lead. Again this proved to be another area of growth for me and gave me an opportunity to meet other colleagues from the Inland Revenue who were practising Christians.

During the early 1970s there were a number of life-changing events for me including of course the arrival of our children. On a spiritual level, however, there were two that stand out in my mind from all the rest. I will take them in the order that they happened, though to me they are of equal significance.

I was admitted to Birmingham General Hospital for an exploratory operation on my left ear. My hearing on that side has always been seriously impaired and it was hoped that a quick look around would reveal the reason, but unfortunately at that time it did not. I was, however, lying in bed following the operation, listening to the hospital radio. My one good ear pricked up when I heard the announcer say that he would shortly be talking with an eccentric hippie American preacher who would be carrying a 12 foot cross into Birmingham's Bull Ring for an evangelistic rally.

As I recall the interview took place over the telephone line, but it was still absolutely riveting stuff. The preacher in question was someone called Arthur Blessitt and he told his story of how he had reached thousands of hippies, prostitutes and drug addicts in the United States with his Jesus message. He had also bought a nightclub on Sunset Strip and turned it into a Christian nightclub, without alcohol and drugs. It was a place where people could meet for a good time without all that other baggage. Arthur told compellingly of how Jesus had spoken to him to carry this 12 foot wooden cross around the world and as he walked the roads he would meet people and tell them about Jesus. He would then very often lead people in a prayer, enabling them to give their lives to Jesus.

Arthur spoke a lot about fun and he became renowned for his extravagant use of 'Jesus stickers'. They were various sizes, but orange and round with messages on them such as Smile God Loves You and New Life in Jesus. He told of the innovative ways that he used the stickers, one being that he would go into a toilet cubicle and unwind the toilet roll, putting his stickers on to the perforations so that when anyone went to the toilet they would get the message Smile Jesus Loves You. He would also go into bookshops and while browsing he would place Gospel tracts inside the books and magazines.

Arthur oozed love for Jesus and everywhere he went he just had to be a witness to that fact. The interview concluded with the information that Arthur would be arriving at Birmingham's Bull Ring the following night along with his wife, four young children and of course the cross.

When Sylvia came to the hospital to visit me later in the day I was full of it. I think she wondered what I had been on. In fact one of Arthur's quips on the interview was that the only pill he takes is the 'Gospill'. He also said that when people call him a nut he just says, "Yes I am a nut but at least I am screwed to the right bolt".

"I've got to get out by tomorrow", I said to Sylvia enthusiastically, "I want to go to the Bull Ring to hear this amazing preacher".

It was November and very cold and the last thing you want to be doing after an ear operation is standing around late at night. Sylvia new I was determined so she went out the next morning and bought me a Parka (longish anorak with a hood that were all the fashion then). I managed to get myself discharged from hospital and duly took my place alongside Sylvia in the Bull Ring. There were several thousand people present. The atmosphere was joyful and there was excitement in the air as we gathered around this large stage that had been erected. At around 7.30pm the gospel band 11.59 came on to stage and sang about half a dozen songs. They were really good, getting us clapping and singing along, and they made quite an impression on me because a year or two later I invited them to come and play at a coffee bar outreach I was running with Sylvia.

Soon the time came for Arthur to step up to the microphone and from the very first syllable he uttered I was hooked. I loved this guy and everything about him. He was like a modern day St Paul, he was radical. Arthur introduced his wife and his children, saying that they nearly always travelled with him and that the kids got their education along the way. Arthur's message about Jesus was plain and simple but so full of fun. I was smitten with Arthur's approach to the Christian faith. Through this long-haired American preacher I fell in love with Jesus in a whole new way. I think this was when and where I first got excited about evangelism. Arthur has now walked with his cross to every nation on this planet and his achievements are now recorded in the Guinness Book of Records as the human being who has done the longest walk in history. ArthurBlessitt.com is now one of my very favourite websites, which I visit at least once a week. He is truly one of the greatest men of faith in ours or any other generation.

Only a few months after that I was to have another truly amazing experience that would stay with me to this very day. I know it may sound strange to some folk, but I have to tell it like it is and that is that I had an encounter with God the Holy Spirit. The Bible calls it Baptism in the Holy Spirit and speaking with tongues, in other words a language that is not your own. If you are so inclined you can read about this in the Bible, Acts of the Apostles, Chapter 2.

Here is a summary of the scriptures in my own words

Following His resurrection Jesus had spoken to His followers that He was going to go away again into Heaven, but that He would send His Holy spirit into the world to be their strength and comforter. Although this concept was hard to understand for the disciples, nevertheless Jesus instructed them to go into Jerusalem and wait there until the Holy Spirit came and filled them with power. Jesus accordingly went back to Heaven (riding on a cloud) and His followers (120 in all including Mary His mother) gathered in an upper room in Jerusalem just as Jesus had directed them to. Eventually, on the day of Pentecost (what we used to call Whit Sunday) the Holy Spirit came like tongues of fire and filled the place where the people were gathered. Immediately they were filled with power and given the ability instantly to speak other languages. From that moment on these people were transformed from being frightened individuals, grieving the loss of their charismatic leader, into bold men and women who went everywhere speaking about Jesus and his resurrection. On that day the Christian Church was born with around 3,000 people surrendering their lives to Jesus Christ.

Getting back to my experience then, Sylvia and I had gone on a weeks' holiday to a Christian House in Sidmouth, North Devon with the idea being that you met with other Christians from around the country and enjoy fellowship. We indulged ourselves with some delicious food, deep conversations and in the morning we would have a short time of worship in singing to God and then have a 'Thought for the Day' given by a guest speaker. In the evenings we would then have another longer meeting with another guest speaker teaching from the Bible. It was good fun and totally different to any holiday we had experienced before.

One of the speakers, Peter Jackson, turned out to be from Birmingham and he was also blind, and we were destined to become very good friends. Peter also had (and still has) a wonderful sense of humour. Apart from regularly telling jokes, he is also very quick-witted and a master of the one-liner. Typically Peter would say "I love throwing people in at the deep end because it makes them dependable". On numerous occasions later I was to discover that to be true personally. Peter has made a large number of piano recordings in a variety of styles initially for Word Records and now on a smaller independent label. You can get more details if interested by doing as I do and visiting his website at Keynote-Ministries.com.

During that week I actually spoke in public for the first time as on one of the evenings I stood up very nervously to explain to people how I had come to know Jesus. At the end of a great week Sylvia and I travelled back to Birmingham on the train and guess who was with us? That's right it was Peter Jackson. For part of the journey Peter was busy brailling letters on his Perkins Brailler, but during one of our conversations when I was telling Peter about Arthur Blessitt in the Bull Ring and of how I would love to have that much confidence, he said to me "What you need is the Baptism of the Holy Spirit". Peter did not say any more however and I did not follow it up, because I had not got a clue what he was talking about.

A few weeks had elapsed when Peter called me on the phone. "Hi John", Peter exclaimed in his usual cheerful manner, "I am preaching at a church near you next Sunday, why don't you and Sylvie come along?"

"Where is it?" I asked with genuine interest.

"Kingstanding Elim Pentecostal Church, Warren Road" came his reply.

"That's where my brother and sister go," I said, "they say it's really lively."

So we arranged to meet Peter there, but not before he had put me under a little pressure by asking me to sit at the front with him for support. I agreed, knowing that Sylvia would sit in the congregation with my brother Paul and sister Susan. It was also a good opportunity to meet Margaret, Peter's wife who brought him by car from their home in Acocks Green.

The night duly arrived and we met Peter and Margaret as arranged in the foyer of the church, a pleasant, modern building accommodating about 300 people. Folk were very friendly as they greeted us with warm handshakes and as we entered the auditorium (for want of a better word) there was some very relaxing music being played softly in the background. Peter and I were taken to the Pastor's office at the back of the church where we had a short chat and prayed together. I was introduced to Pastor Morrison, a warm-hearted Irishman, about 60 years of age I guess with a rasping Belfast accent. He said he would lead the service and then hand over to Peter at an appropriate point. Out in the main church area we could already hear the joyful sound of Gospel choruses being sung with great vigour.

We duly took our seats and about 20 minutes into the service Peter turned to me and dropped his bombshell. "It would be really good if you could just in a few sentences tell the people how you came to know Jesus and just what he means to you".

My heart seemed to sink into my boots and I began to sweat profusely. I protested to Peter that I felt very nervous, but he just said that was natural and that I would be fine. Peter was then taken to sit at the piano and he began to speak.

"Good evening everyone and it's great to be back with you at Warren Road. Before I play a piece for you however, I want to introduce you to a young man by the name of John Flanner who is going to share with you about how he became a Christian. I stood up and Pastor Morrison came across and led me to the microphone. I was incredibly nervous but felt I did okay in talking for two minutes before so many people. At least they did give me a clap when I had finished and it was then back to Peter who came out with that priceless line about throwing people in at the deep end.

After Peter had finished playing and preaching it was left to Pastor Morrison to bring the service to a close, but not before he had given a plug for the church prayer meeting to be held the following Thursday. He said that it would be a special meeting to pray for people to be baptised in the Holy Spirit. Peter nudged me and said, "Be there, that's for you – remember our chat on the train".

Thursday night came around very quickly and Sylvia and I walked to the church with my brother and sister and a few of their young friends. On arrival we were told that the prayer meeting was in the room round the back of the church and once there we took our seats near the back. There were about 10 rows with something like 15 seats in each row. In all I suppose about 40 people gathered on that night for the prayer meeting.

After a couple of hymns and a few other songs Pastor Morrison read some verses from the Bible and then explained what Baptism in the Holy Spirit was all about. He told us about Jesus' disciples being very afraid after his death, fearing that they too may be crucified. Once the Holy Spirit had filled them, however, there was no fear anymore and each person discovered they had been given a gift of being able to speak in other languages. It is recorded that on that day, the 'Day of Pentecost', some 3,000 people gave their lives to Jesus and many were healed of their diseases.

Pastor Morrison further explained that the same power was still available today to anyone who was hungry and thirsty for it. He asked people who were timid about admitting they were followers of Jesus to come forward for prayer. Sylvia and I went forward and stood at the front along with about a dozen others.

We were encouraged by Pastor Morrison to just begin to praise the Lord. I did not know what that meant but as I listened to others saying audibly "praise the Lord", "Hallelujah", "I love you Jesus" and the like I soon got the idea. I began very quietly saying "I love you Jesus" until one of the other church leaders came to me and encouraged me to be a little bolder and not so quiet.

Over and over again I began saying Hallelujah until I was struggling to get the word out. It was as if my tongue had been tied up, the word just would not come. Then all of a sudden my tongue was loosed and out of my mouth came a language I had never heard before. It just flowed like a river from deep within me and it was oh so exhilarating. There was so much joy flooding my being, this was ecstasy. I was a bit surprised therefore when someone came to me and asked me then to be quiet for a moment and sit down.

He said into my ear, "I have asked you to do that because this is a gift that God has given you and with all gifts you can use it whenever you wish to do so."

It was explained to me that this was a good gift. I had control over it and not it over me. When something evil comes into our lives it seeks to control us but with God He does not take away our free will. Well I went home that night on the proverbial cloud nine and in all honesty I don't think I have ever really come down since. That same Holy Spirit is still with me and even in the darkest and most testing of times I know that joy is still on the inside.

Just in case you are wondering, Sylvia did not get the same as me that night, but a few weeks later at another church, she went through a similar, if not identical experience. That is an important point to make. We are all individuals and God knows exactly the right way to meet with us. All that He requires is that we are hungry and thirsty for him. In essence therefore that is the night I believe I really began to step out of fear and into faith, leaving behind the negative experiences and the hold they had over me for all those years. The new John Flanner was about to emerge from the shadows.

Turn on and tune in

Music has always been a big part of my life and one artist who has had quite an impact on my life, particularly in those formative years of my Christian faith is the late great Johnny Cash. Three of his works caused me to exercise my faith in most unexpected ways. Firstly, Johnny himself financed the making of a film called *The Gospel Road* which told the story of Jesus with Johnny himself narrating words straight from the Bible. Johnny's wife June played the part of Mary Magdalene in the movie which contained some great songs, but sadly as far as I am aware, has never been shown on the big screen or on television in the UK. When it was first made available in the UK however I managed to hire a copy for a month and together with a few friends we took it on the road to show it in churches, schools, a prison and even to a couple of Country and Western clubs which were held in pubs.

One of the latter venues was at The Roebuck Pub in Erdington, Birmingham where the Silver Saddle Country and Western Club used to meet. At the end of the film a man came up to me to say how much he had enjoyed it and telling me that it had brought tears to his eyes. He said that it reminded him of the time he had given his life to Jesus many years before at a Sunday school in Truro, Cornwall where he came from. This man's name was Tony Buzza, he was an avid fan of Roy Rogers and what I neglected to say was that he was dressed in all of the cowboy gear including the gun, safely tucked away in the holster I am glad to say.

It was a memorable month in which many lives were touched, however at the end of it I suddenly ended up in hospital suffering from viral meningitis. I remember my head hurting so badly and all I could hear were the words of Johnny Cash *So come along with me and I'll take you in the footsteps of Jesus as we travel along the gospel road..."*

Secondly I remember being very challenged by the words of one of Johnny's songs contained on an album I had just purchased. The song, if it is right to call it that because it was more of a monologue, was I think called *Dear Mrs*. It told the story of a guy in prison who each morning looked out from his cell as the letters were delivered only to be disappointed day after day and year after year

98

because of no letter. Every time I listened to it I felt a stirring inside as if I should do something.

As it happened I knew someone through attending the lunchtime services at St Philip's Cathedral. Don Bissell was a senior Probation Officer in Birmingham and so I contacted him with my thoughts and asked him if he could give me some advice. It turned out that he ran volunteer courses from his office in Birmingham for people who wanted to get involved in prison visiting or writing to prisoners. I then attended the six one hour meetings at Don's office and eventually was assigned a prisoner to write to which I did until his release and integration back into the community.

Finally, Sylvia read a book to me which was entitled *The New Johnny Cash*. It was a biographical account of Johnny's life and particularly how he had rediscovered his Christian faith through the love of his wife June Carter. I loved that book and it touched me so deeply and I wanted everyone to enjoy it. On what was then BBC Radio Birmingham there was a country music show called Sounds Country presented by Ken Dudeney. I was a regular listener and wrote to Ken telling him about the book with my usual enthusiasm and recommending that he review it on his show one week.

Well to my surprise Ken rang me at home one night and suggested that it would be far better if I went into the studio to review the book myself on the programme. I was very excited but still a little on the nervous side as I made my way on two buses across the city to the Pebble Mill studios. Ken met me at reception and to use a modern word, he was gobsmacked to discover that I could not see. I had not thought to mention it in my letter and I later discovered that Ken was wondering how I would read my script. I reassured Ken that I would be okay and just ad lib. Well my little spot was recorded and to be truthful it was a good job because I made a right mess of it. I think I was so keen to talk about Jesus that I actually forgot to review the book.

Over a coffee afterwards however I did manage to talk with Ken about my love of country gospel music and a few weeks later he asked me if I would play six of my favourite Country Gospel tracks and talk about what they mean to me. He thought that would be a great and slightly unusual show for Easter week. This was a dream come true for me, to have the opportunity to indulge myself by playing some of my favourite songs on the radio and then talking about the spiritual significance of them was such an incredible privilege. I played a song called *I Know* by Wanda Jackson that created a lot of interest with people calling in to know where they could get hold of the album from which it was taken. Also an elderly, housebound lady wrote in and sent a small amount of money earmarked for the young man who played the music to give to his favourite charity. From that moment on I had a regular monthly spot on the show to play Country Gospel tracks.

A few years later the station underwent some major policy changes, including changing its name to Radio WM. The specialist music programmes such as country, folk, jazz etc., were dropped in favour of more generic and mainly speech-based programmes. I was retained however and given the opportunity to assist Michael Blood on his Sunday morning religious programme, then called *A Word in Advance*. I was able to go in, again on a monthly basis, to review the latest Christian record releases. I did that all told for about 12 years until music was dropped almost entirely from the station. Michael and I got on really well together and listeners used to love our little chats about this, that and the other. Basically I would just respond to Michael's questions by telling stories of what God was doing in my life just as I am doing in this book.

I really love radio on both sides of the microphone and would love to have the opportunity of getting back into it again one day. When eventually I get to heaven therefore and I hear those immortal words "Hello I'm Johnny Cash", I will respond by thanking him for his life and music, which God has used to open up some exciting doors for me.

There have been many occasions when I believe God has spoken to me through the radio and prompted me to take action in some way and I want to share some of these with you. One morning while listening to the local news my attention was grabbed by news of a car accident quite local to where I was living. I heard that a young lady had to be cut from her car and was taken to Solihull Hospital where after surgery she had lost part of her left hand. Her name was Karen and I was immediately moved with compassion to pray for her. The Birmingham Evening Mail that day had a report on the crash and actually named the road where Karen lived with her parents. I wrote a letter to Karen, letting her know that I was praying for her and that Jesus really loved her so much, then having obtained the address from the telephone directory we posted it off to her. It was several weeks later that I heard from Karen's Dad saying how much she had appreciated the letter and what encouragement it had given her. Gladly the last I heard she was making a good recovery.

I think my most dramatic night of radio listening, however, came on 29th May 1985. Liverpool Football club were to play the European Cup Final against Italian champions Juventus at the Heysal Stadium in Brussels. I was listening to the build up to the game with the commentary team of Peter Jones, Mike Ingham and summariser Emlyn Hughes when suddenly a horrific picture began to unfold. Marauding Liverpool supporters had caused a wall to collapse leading to the deaths of 39 people in the mayhem that ensued. The commentators struggled to hold back the tears as they described what they were seeing an hour or so before the match was due to begin.

The match eventually got under way but with the stench of death in the air it was all a massive anti-climax and though Juventus won the game 1-0 nobody really cared. The beautiful game lost many friends that night and the United Kingdom with its reputation for football hooliganism had made many more enemies around the world. That night I lay prostrate on the lounge carpet shedding many tears for those who had lost their lives and for the low state that our country had now sunk to. I felt so ashamed and at that moment I felt I would never again attend another football match. I wanted to disassociate myself from the thugs who were invading our great game and destroying the reputation of our country.

In the days that followed my heartfelt prayer was "God what can we do?" When Sunday came around I was at church, lost in worshipping God when suddenly I felt what I can only describe as a surging from my stomach. Emotion was rising within me and a phrase came to my mind very strongly and it was "Let your voice be heard above that of the heathen". I knew this all related to the football in some way. I think that cry came from deep within me to God to let His voice be heard above all the other political and religious voices who were trotting out the same old platitudes such as "Bring back the birch", "Bring back national service", "Lock them up and throw away the key" etc. Along with many others I am sure I desperately wanted God to act. However, it was almost as if God turned the statement back on me and said "I live in you by the power of my Holy Spirit so now let your voice be heard above that of the heathen".

I decided to go for it and go along with the old maxim that nobody can change the whole world but each of us can change somebody's world. As you already know I am a devoted follower of Aston Villa. Even at my beloved Villa Park, our home ground, the atmosphere had been getting ugly at times with aggression, hate-filled and obscene chanting becoming more commonplace. I therefore put together a little strategy to improve things and put my suggestions in a letter to the then Commercial Manager, Tony Stevens.

A few days after sending my letter Tony called me on the phone and said that he would like to meet with me at his office to discuss my ideas further. A day or two later I was at Villa Park and sitting in Tony's office drinking tea served in china cups as I outlined my proposals. From my perspective I wanted the club to give me permission to start up an Aston Villa Christian Supporters Association. We would meet before every home game in a local church to pray about the atmosphere on the terraces. We would pray for peace, harmony and fun at the ground and for it to be a safe place for families to come along. We would also pray for a positive atmosphere to be present in the ground as well as for new levels of sportsmanship between the players. In addition, if our credibility was sustained, then we could also pray for people within the club who were going through difficult times, especially players with career-threatening injuries. Among a number of other suggestions I made was that when the two teams come out on to the field they should actually come out together side by side, as they had always done in the FA Cup final, and even be seen talking and joking together. In that way the players would emerge from the tunnel to a chorus of cheers rather than a mixture, thereby starting off proceedings with a positive atmosphere.

Well would you believe it, when the fixtures came out for the new season Aston Villa's first home game was against Liverpool. The Club agreed to my request and the teams did come out side by side and now it is done like that at all games. I can't say for definite, but I think that was the first time it had been done in a normal league game and now it is the accepted practice.

The Club and in particular Chairman Doug Ellis were extremely supportive of our venture and the then manager, Graham Turner was always available to chat and help out whenever he could. In fact Graham's wife, Anne would often attend our prayer meetings with her two young sons. The numbers attending those prayer meetings were not great by any means, but they were effective and powerful and in that first season Aston Villa won an award for having the most sporting and well behaved supporters.

Our venture attracted quite a bit of media interest and it transpired that a number of other prayer groups formed around the country to get behind their clubs too. The Aston Villa prayer group continued for about four seasons and eventually folded after I had moved out of the area and my successor John Gosnall (who did a wonderful job) collapsed and died very suddenly. Just maybe the prayer group had run its course.

So next time you turn your radio or television news on, listen for the heart of God and be open to what He would have you do or say. He will probably take you out of your comfort zone, but at least it will be an adventure.

Living by faith

In the Bible (John Chapter 3) there is an account of Jesus having a chat with a man by the name of Nicodemus one night. Nicodemus was a very religious man, a devout Jew, but he came to Jesus enquiring what he must do to get eternal life. It is in this conversation where Jesus says "You must be born again" something which has become an in phrase in our generation. Jesus, however, was talking about a spiritual rebirth.

In the narrative (and this is something I love) Jesus says that the person who is born of the Spirit is like the wind in that no one knows where it comes from and no one knows where it is going to. That speaks to me of a glorious freedom and of an incredible unpredictability that should be the hallmark of every Christian. Christians, I believe should be on the biggest high and get the greatest buzz from life of any people on the Planet. No need whatsoever to take artificial stimuli such as alcohol or drugs when you have the Son of God living on the inside of you.

So it was that after that experience of being filled up with the Holy Spirit and speaking in tongues I set off with an expectation of God being with me and that I was on planet Earth to represent (or more accurately re-present) Jesus. I truly believe that I am God's gift to women and to men and to boys and girls, but then so are you. Created in the image of God, full of exciting potential.

On the subject of boys and girls, we were sitting down for tea one night when a friend from church called to see us. John Place, saddened by a recent divorce had become a regular visitor to our home. He enjoyed our company (and Sylvia's cooking) and he was great with the kids.

John said, somewhat tongue in cheek, "There are a crowd of young children playing outside your house, maybe you could start a Christian club for them".

Though it was said in such a light-hearted way, it actually turned out to be God's will for our lives at that time. We had just finished reading a book called *Take My Home* and it was all about different people who had seen their home as a gift from God and had dedicated it to God's service. Now just maybe we had heard the voice of God through our friend.

After praying about this with a few people and giving the matter careful consideration we decided to launch a club called One Way Special, Jesus being the one way to Heaven according to his own words "I am the way, the truth and the life; no one can come to the Father except through me". We adopted a little song called One Way Jesus Christ as our theme tune which was taken from an album by a local Christian band called Dave Pope and the Alethians.

We set a date for it to start on Mondays from 6pm to 7pm and we planned activities such as singing, Bible quizzes, memory verse challenges and stories with a Gospel message done either by me or by a visiting speaker. We would also run a shop where the kids could trade in tokens, which they would receive for attendance, bringing their Bibles, inviting friends, answers to questions in the quiz, good behaviour etc. One Way Special was aimed at children between the ages of 7 to 11 and I wrote letters to all the parents explaining who we were and saying that it was basically a Christian Sunday school, but on a Monday night in our home.

We started with 12 kids and very quickly we were averaging around 30 each week. After a few months things really started to take off and numbers started to increase dramatically week by week so we had to move out from our house and hire a local community centre. We reached our peak one week when we had 180 children by which time we had built up a good team of helpers from various local churches to assist with the music, teaching, register and maintaining discipline. They were amazing, heady times and though it was tiring it was also extremely rewarding to be sowing this good seed into these young lives. The cost of doing all of this of course was fairly substantial with the

Top left: Me as a child in 1949.

Top right: Aged 11, and the love affair with football had already started.

Bottom left: A family photo with all my siblings - me aged 12, Joan aged 10, Paul aged 5 and Susan aged 2.

Bottom right: Here I am aged 19 training to live as a blind person at Manor House, Torquay in 1967.

Aged 19 outside my family home in Erdington, having recently been diagnosed as suffering with Leber's Optic Atrophy in 1967.

Top left: Sylvia and I on our wedding day at
St Margaret's Church, Erdington on 29th November 1969.

Top right: The Flanner family, clockwise from top:
Allison, Me, Ian, Sylvia, Beverley and Sara.

Bottom left: The twins at The Sorrento Maternity Unit,
Moseley.

Bottom right: Ian aged 6 in his Aston Villa football strip.

Our family at Walsgrave Drive, at the time of the *Encounter* programme in 1983.

Speaking at Malvern High School in 1983. (Picture courtesy of Central TV *It's A Gift*).

Nicholas Attard and I at Harvest Bible College, Cornwall.

On the radio waves at BBC Radio Plymouth in 1989.

Ian and I at the FA Cup Final at Wembley Arena, 2000.

Receiving the first ever Civil Service Diversity and Equality Award in 2006.
(left to right) Rageh Omaar, Me, Sir Gus O'Donnell and Paul Gray.

Sylvia and I relaxing at Rum Point, Cayman Islands.

On holiday in Florida with Carole and Paul Crabtree.

The Flanner family at a recent celebration - (left to right) Beverley, Allison, Sylvia, John, Sara and Ian.

Outside the Town Hall in my beloved Birmingham in 2008.

hire of the hall, materials, and paying speakers and so on, so I must let you in on the way in which God wonderfully provided.

Sylvia and I were baptised together by total immersion at Kingstanding Elim Church in Birmingham on Sunday 13th February 1972 along with about six other people. As part of the service all of the people being baptised were required to explain to the congregation why it was they were taking that step to make their faith public in that way. We were all very nervous, myself included. During my little testimony I had said something to the effect that Sylvia and I loved Jesus and we were using our home in order to make Jesus known to children and teenagers. We were already providing our house every Friday evening for several of my brother's teenage friends to come in and have supper and discuss matters of faith. At the end of the service a businessman came up to me and said that he had never been to such a service before and that he had found it deeply moving. He also said that he was a Christian and he had just set up a charity in which he would give money and provide materials for any work that was involved in sharing God's love with children and young people. He said if there was anything we needed then or in the future then I had only to ask.

A few weeks later this kind man, by the name of Bob Perry, arranged for a piano to be delivered to our house so that we could have music at our meetings and he set up an open account for me to go into a Christian bookshop in Birmingham to purchase anything I wanted for the young people and later for the children who came to One Way Special. Bob became good friends with us for many years and though we have not seen each other in a long time now, I do know that he is living happily in Tiverton, Devon with his wife Janet. This 'divine appointment' with Bob now set the tone for our walk with God as we had seen him act in financial provision in such an unexpected way. In books we were reading about how God provided for those who are prepared to step out on a limb and trust Him, so we determined to try and live in that way ourselves.

Our home was open to children on a Monday night, teenagers on a Friday night and we regularly saw them giving their lives to Jesus just as we had done. They were thrilling days, but hard too with a young family ourselves to contend with.

I made reference to this earlier, but even though Sylvia and I were the driving force behind this work on the housing estate, God raised up a wonderful team of people to support and be there for us and I will always be appreciative to each of them for that. On occasions when things got too much for Sylvia and me a number of these people were there for us with words of encouragement and arms around the shoulder where necessary. On one occasion we were at our wits end not knowing how we could pay our electric bill when one of the helpers Christine rang up from work to ask if we had a need. Sylvia and I were at that very moment discussing (arguing would be more precise) as to how we were going to pay the bill. Never one to hide things for very long (I'm no actor, I wear my heart on my sleeve), I said to Christine,

"That's amazing, how did you know?"

"Know what", she replied, "God just put you on my heart and so I have rung you."

I told Christine that Sylvia and I had just been having a 'slight disagreement' over how we could pay the electric bill when we did not have the money. Christine asked me how much it was and then said she would drop the cash round after work. It was very humbling to have to learn to receive in that way but at that time we were extremely grateful to God for putting it into Christine's mind to ring and appreciative that she was obedient in doing what she felt God wanted her to do.

It was around this time that I started to feel very pressured in terms of time. I had a wife and three young children plus a job where I was working 40 hours a week. In addition we were seeking to be faithful in attending meetings of our local church and running two meetings in our home together with the follow up work which was involved. For instance some of the children would like to come around after school and talk about issues going on in their lives.

I began to pray earnestly about this feeling that we would have to give up the work with the children and the teenagers. Increasingly, however, I began to sense that God was saying that it would be my job at the Inland Revenue that would have to go. My first thought was that it was crazy to think like that. Finances were tight as it was without giving up my job to work for God with no regular income. However the thought persisted and even grew stronger. Verses in the Bible kept jumping out at me about living by faith, trusting in God and whenever we went to church meetings it seemed like that was the subject.

We had just read a book called God smuggler, which is the story of a Dutch guy called Brother Andrew, who had spent much of his adult life smuggling Bibles into countries where they were banned. As Andrew's story unfolded it was thrilling to read the way in which God provided for all of his needs, often over and above what he could have imagined.

All of this served to make me unsettled at work and desirous of being obedient to God. It took me six months of God being on my case before I was eventually able to type out my notice of resignation. I rang Sylvia to tell her that I had at last done it and we were both so relieved, full of joy and at peace once again.

At that stage I have to say that our biggest concern was how we would pay the rent on our Council house. Mum and Dad lived just down the road so if we ran out of food we could always go knocking on their door, but paying the rent and other bills that was something else. We need not have worried however because God had gone ahead of us and answered our prayers in a way that we could not have imagined.

The day after finishing my job as an audio typist with the Inland Revenue, Sylvia and I together with our three small children (all under the age of 2) set off with some friends of our from church for a week's holiday at Pontins Holiday Camp in Blackpool. It was not the usual sort of Pontins holiday because this was a week-long conference of the Elim Pentecostal Church and it involved meetings for all ages through the day and night as well. We had a great time that week with our friends Brian and Janet with their four young children.

Once the holiday was over we all returned to Birmingham, Brian went back to the welding business with his brother in law, whilst I was about to take up a new full time role caring for people on the Wyrley Birch Housing Estate and trusting God to unfold each day according to His perfect will.

On arriving home from Blackpool we saw God's handiwork straightaway and it concerned the rent which we had been so concerned about. We had a letter from the Birmingham Housing Department explaining that they were sending us a cheque for just in excess of £200 in respect of unclaimed rent rebate stretching back over the previous year and in addition for the next six months our rent would be 48 pence per week, which they would require us to pay fortnightly. I can't tell you the great sense of joy and relief that we felt at that point. It was incredible news and Sylvia and I agreed that though our faith was small it did run to trusting God for 48 pence a week in order to cover the rent.

Over the course of the next few years we saw God provide for all our needs in some most remarkable ways. All this time we were continuing to have the children coming along for One Way Special on a Monday night, the teenagers (up to 40 of them) in our house every Friday night for bible study and a little supper.

We also had the occasional coffee mornings for the elderly and I started to deliver a Christian newspaper called Challenge to about 200 homes on the Estate. My mind went back in time to when I was 13 years of age when I used to have a newspaper round on that very estate. I loved delivering the news to people's homes then but now I was delivering the good news about Jesus and I loved that even more.

I think a number of people were more than a little shocked to find a blind person undertaking this kind of work. I didn't mind that however because there is something about me now that quite likes to surprise people. I've continued to do that down through the years and why not? Although in myself I am very ordinary, living on the inside of me I have an extraordinarily amazing God.

I remember one Monday night when I was feeling really tired I just did not feel like leading One Way Special. Even with our wonderful team of helpers, it took a lot of exuberant energy to participate with the children in some of the lively songs, quizzes and Bible stories which often had to be dramatised in order to get the attention of the kids. After One Way Special had finished I was then driven by my friend, John Place, to Cannon Street Baptist Church in Handsworth where I was to give a 30 minute talk to a ladies group about the work we were doing on the estate.

I could not have felt less like it and I had to pray and ask the Holy Spirit to flow through me in order to inspire my audience, which consisted of about 20, mainly elderly ladies, though I recall a few male members of the church did sneak in.

Well God did help me enormously and His presence filled the small room in which we were gathered. At the end of the meeting following a short prayer from the Minister, people came up and shook my hand warmly and most said that God had spoken to them and as a result they wanted to give me money. Coins and notes were being stuffed into my jacket pockets by all and sundry to the point where I was quite bewildered by it all. John was quite amused by the proceedings and as he drove me home to Sylvia he was chuckling to himself most of the way.

When we arrived home we told Sylvia what had happened as we counted the money. In all there was just over £40 on a night and that was a lot of money back in the mid-1970s. This ensured that we would not have to go cap in hand to Mum and Dad for a week or two at least.

This phase of my life was of course very different to anything I had known before. No regular income, no set pattern to my day and nobody telling me what to do etc. Sylvia enjoyed having me around to help a little with the children and I liked that too. However God had called me to work for him and I learned to build discipline into my life and create a whole new framework for myself. Having said that I was becoming very concerned about an ugly side to my character that had started to manifest itself.

Temper temper!

Throughout my life I had never really displayed much of a temper, even when being kicked on the football field. When the children would wake up at night however and not go back to sleep I found that very annoying. Particularly when the twins were babies it was as if they had night and day mixed up. They would sleep in the day and then lie awake crying throughout the night. Given that we were in a first floor maisonette at the time this was increasingly difficult for us as there were neighbours either side and underneath.

It became a pressure cooker situation trying to keep them quiet so that the neighbours would not be disturbed, whilst at the same time desperately needing rest ourselves. It was then I think that I discovered I had a threshold beyond which lay a very nasty temper.

On one occasion Sylvia and I were in Torquay with our three small children and we were having a heated exchange of views. I felt myself getting increasingly tense until Sylvia said something which I did not like and I lashed out with my hand and slapped her around the face. Immediately blood began to pour out of her nose and the children were horrified at what I had done and so was I of course. Ironically within seconds a photographer came up to us and asked if we would like him to take a happy family photograph. You can guess what Sylvia's reply was I'm sure!

As if that wasn't bad enough a short while later back home in Birmingham, it was around teatime one night, the kids were all ready for bed, having been in the bath and dressed in their pyjamas. I was getting ready to go out and give my Christian testimony at a remand home for girls about 25 miles away. A friend of our by the name of Denis Guest was picking me up in his car. Denis would preach at this event, I would give my testimony of how I came to know Jesus and two sisters by the names of Sue and Carol would sing two or three songs.

Unfortunately a few minutes before Denis was due to arrive, something triggered off another argument between Sylvia and me. It was horrible and again it led to me lashing out and this time Sylvia fell back on to the floor as she tried to avoid my blow. If she had banged her head she could have been killed and the whole scene was horrendous as the doorbell rang.

Sylvia, understandably shouted, "Go off to your religious meeting and don't bother to come back."

I went to the door and as we were already running late, Denis was back at the car. I got in and we drove away. We had not gone more than a few minutes when I began to cry. I told Denis what had gone on and he pulled over to the side of the road, stopped the car and prayed there and then for Sylvia and me.

Denis encouraged me to believe that God had something good in store that night at the remand home and even though I felt totally unworthy to be out representing a God of love, Denis reminded me that we are all sinners saved by God's amazing grace. He said that I should give it my best shot and then when we arrived home later in the evening he would come in and talk with Sylvia and me. We duly arrived at the remand home and it turned out to be a great night with 12 of the teenage girls giving their lives to Jesus.

On arriving back home Denis did as he said he would and came in to pray with us, but Sylvia had actually gone off to bed so in the end we just prayed about the situation downstairs before Denis headed off home.

A short while later, however, we went away for a week's holiday in a cottage on a farm near Port Isaac in Cornwall. We were with our friends Brian and Janet

Davis and their four kids and overall we had a very good time. Sylvia however was still emotionally raw from recent events and she would take herself off to bed at about 8pm each night. I felt embarrassed and awkward about this for I knew that our friends would be wondering what the problem was.

On one particular evening after Sylvia had gone to bed and while Brian and Janet were busy in the kitchen, I was reading part of my Braille Bible. I read a verse which said "Confess your faults to one another and you shall be healed". As I read those words I knew that I needed to go and confess to my friends what I had done to Sylvia. I went into the kitchen where Brian and Janet were preparing food for the next day.

"Hi John" said Brian, "how's Sylvie?"

"That's what I want to talk with you about" I said, before breaking down in floods of tears.

Brian, a big man in every sense of the word, immediately left the sink and came over to me.

I blurted out, "Brian, I think I'm demon-possessed because I keep on hitting Sylvia."

Brian held me tight in a bear hug for several minutes as we sobbed deeply in each other's arms. When words eventually came, Brian did not condemn me or ask any questions, but simply prayed a blessing over me following which I felt totally clean.

In the days that followed Janet was able to chat with Sylvia and release some of her pent up anger and confusion. As for me that verse in the Bible "Confess your faults one to another and you shall be healed" must be true because I have never lashed out at Sylvia again since that time. If you are reading this and you have a problem with your temper let me encourage you to be open about sharing that with someone you love and trust, or if it is perceived to be a serious problem then go and get professional help. Do not be too proud. As I see it, it is every bit as much a disability as me being blind.

The power of prayer

It was in those days that I developed the habit of getting up early in the morning (6am) to spend time in prayer and reading from my Braille Bible. When you have no money coming in on a regular salary it's amazing how that motivates you to focus on God and His Word. As well as placing our needs as a family before God every morning I would also look to Him to guide me each day with regard to what I should be doing. Sometimes it was visiting the elderly in their homes, sometimes delivering the *Challenge* newspaper and sometimes preparing for the children's or the teenagers' meetings. On other occasions it might mean meeting with other Christians in the locality, or going to speak at a meeting somewhere or other. It was all very thrilling to see the way in which God mapped out the days and created the openings for me.

Through delivering the *Challenge* newspaper around the housing estate I got to know many people, but among the most interesting were Bobby and Sylvia Evans. They were Christians and a very cheerful pair. Our three little daughters loved them because they were so jovial. Bobby was a dwarf (no more than 3 foot tall) whilst Sylvia, his wife, was about 6 foot in height so you can imagine what they looked like. It was a wonderful sight to behold when Bobby would jump into the shopping trolley and Sylvia would wheel him along the road.

It was teatime in the Flanner household one magical night just before Christmas when there was a knock at the door. I went to answer the door, to find Sylvia and Bobby there, but before I could welcome them in Bobby had nipped around me and was into the lounge playfully teasing the children with talk of Father Christmas coming soon. He wasn't far wrong in that Sylvia (not mine, but Bobby's girl) wheeled the aforementioned shopping trolley minus Bobby on this occasion, into the kitchen, where she found my Sylvia slaving over a hot stove. This could get confusing, but Sylvia said to Sylvia, "God has been talking to Bobby and me about your needs this Christmas, so we have done something about it".

With that Bobby's Sylvia proceeded to unzip the top of the trolley to reveal a bag jammed full of all kinds of foodstuff. Everything you could imagine for a week's family shopping was included in there plus a few little surprises for the kids. There was an abundant supply of tights for my Sylvia and the thing we remember to this day, there were 800 tea bags. My reputation had obviously gone before me. There was even a Christmas pudding and a small box of Christmas crackers.

Needless to say, we had indeed been praying about various needs that we had at that festive season and it was typical that God should respond in such an extravagant manner. Bobby and Sylvia always said that it was well worth the expense to see the look of incredulity and wonder upon our faces. Beverley, Sara and Allison, young as they were, fully entered into the excitement of the occasion too.

During these years I have to say that we really looked forward to seeing the postman, always wondering if he was carrying another miracle or two in his bag for us. From the time the postman delivered the letter from the Council Housing Department telling us we had been offered the very house we had requested, right up to the present time we have fond memories of God doing some amazing things and using the postman as his delivering angel.

I was then working as a self-employed person, purchasing my own National Insurance stamp. I had to keep records of income and expenditure for the Inland Revenue. With regard to the income I split that into two categories, fees and gifts. The fees are what I earned for speaking engagements, which wasn't much. The gifts were the amazing amount of donations that were either handed to us at Church or what came in the post and many of these gifts were anonymous too. Financial gifts ranging from £1 up to £500 came our way via many different people, who all had one thing in common, they were directed by God to do so and from our point of view we were extremely thankful for their obedience. True we went through times of lack and we also went through times of abundance and it was a difficult balancing act knowing when to spend and when to save, when to give out to others and when to withhold. If anything we tended to err on the carefree (prefer that to careless) side of things.

During one particularly difficult time when money was scarce I remember praying really hard about money we needed to pay a gas bill and I was also aware that we needed a holiday. Indeed it was our family GP who had spoken to me and sensitively brought the conversation around to make me aware that Sylvia needed a break.

As I prayed earnestly about these matters a strange thing began to happen. Every time I prayed about these issues in my mind's eye I could see my collection of pop singles. They were my pride and joy and there were around 700 of them. It took me a while to realise what was going on, but it soon became apparent that God was asking me to sell my beloved record collection. The thought was too painful to contemplate and I tried to push it out of my mind but day after day the thought would not go away. Then one day my brother Paul came to our home to look for a particular record which he wanted to borrow. Quite spontaneously as he was browsing he asked, "I don't suppose you would consider selling any of these would you?"

"No way" was my immediate response.

However, after Paul had gone, having found what it was he wanted, I could not get his question out of my mind. It troubled me for days and I came to the conclusion that this was probably God's way of answering part of my prayer. The upshot was that Paul purchased half of my record collection for £50 and that more than paid for the gas bill. It almost broke my heart, but worse was to follow.

As I prayed further about the holiday matter I felt again that God was saying I should get rid of the rest of the records. Eventually I decided I had better co-operate with my Lord and went to a local dealer and sold them raising enough money to book a week's holiday for the family. I even got rid of all the albums as well thinking, "If God wants all of me then all of me he can have".

I have since learned of course that that is what God wants. He gave himself totally for me and He wants nothing less in return. Having said that I have also discovered that you can never out-give God. I have also become aware that if God asks you to give something up for him, it is only because he wants to replace it with something far better. Later, through my friend Peter Jackson, himself then a recording artist with Word Records, I was given the opportunity of presenting Discovery evenings in homes and churches.

What this was in effect was an opportunity to promote Word Records by going to homes and churches and before an invited group of people play tracks from the latest Christian record releases. I would take along a selection of discs that people could purchase at the end of the evening if they so wished. I was then allowed 30% commission on all I sold, to plough back into the work on the Housing Estate, so here again we saw God's wonderful provision.

All of this of course led to me having quite an extensive knowledge of the Christian gospel music scene and stood me in good stead for the time when I would get an invitation to play this kind of music on BBC Radio Birmingham initially and then later Radio WM with Ken Dudeney and Michael Blood. The old hymn writer got it bang on when he penned those words *God moves in a mysterious way his wonders to perform.*

I have thoroughly enjoyed my experiences in broadcasting. Apart from working on radio in Birmingham, I have also featured on local radio stations in Leicester, Devon and Cornwall over the years. I had an exciting opportunity to share something of my life story and faith in God on a Christian radio station called *Heaven 97* in the Cayman Islands and that led to me receiving an invitation to preach at a church in Grand Cayman called Faith Deliverance Centre. That was a wonderful experience with Sylvia and I being the only white people in a congregation of over 100. The place was rocking with the sound of praises to God as people from mainly a Jamaican background gave vent to their joy at being saved.

At the end of that service the Pastor of the church encouraged his congregation to come up to me and show their appreciation. I can honestly say that I have never been hugged and kissed by so many people in such a short space of time, I felt loved well and truly. What we were doing in the Cayman Island, I'll tell you later, but for now let's just say it was another one of God's 'little' surprises.

It's not just on radio that I have been able to talk about my faith either. The God of surprises that I have come to know and love had another one in store for me when I received a phone call from a man by the name of Bernard Cartwright at Central Television. Bernard said that he worked as a researcher on religious programming for Central TV and that a friend of his by the name of Jill had told

him about my work for a local church. Jill suffered from multiple sclerosis and it is true that I used to visit her at home and pray with her and from time to time Sylvia and I would also go round in the evening when Jill's charming French husband was home from work and he would treat us to red wine and French brie cheese. That incidentally was our introduction to this savoury delicacy, which we have since come to greatly appreciate.

Apparently Jill had told Bernard a lot about me and I must have intrigued him sufficiently enough for him to give me a call and in true researcher style, Bernard proceeded to ask penetrating questions about my life, attitude and beliefs. He said he would talk with his boss and get back to me and let me know if they were going to make a programme.

Only a couple of days slipped by before Bernard was back on the phone saying that it was looking promising and that he needed to come to my house for a chat. The idea was put to me that they would like me to take part in a 15 minute interview for a programme called *Come Close* which would go out across the Midlands on Central TV late on a Monday night, as it turned out after the darts coverage. I would be interviewed by a man by the name of Stuart White about my faith in God and how as a blind person I could believe in a God of love and so on. It was also explained to me that although the programme was to be recorded, it had to be done in one take because they were on a tight budget and they could not afford any more studio time. I even had to sign a contract agreeing to abide by certain criteria.

It was exciting however going up to the studios in Birmingham and being made up with face powder to look as if I had a wonderful tan. Although I was very nervous about doing the programme it all went pretty well as I talked about my life and adjusting to being a blind person. I also demonstrated how to use the white stick and some of the equipment I have for writing Braille, writing cheques, playing games like scrabble and dominoes etc.

The interview must have been well received because a month or two later I received another phone call from Central TV. This time it was from Michael Hart (brother of the famous television artist Tony Hart). Michael, who I believe was the senior producer in religious broadcasting at the time on Central, said that following the success of *Come Close* they were now considering me as a subject for one of their *Encounter* documentaries. *Encounter* was a 30 minute show that originally went out on a Sunday evening but was then showing at 2pm on Sunday afternoons, just before *Star Soccer*, as it was in the Midlands then. This sounded even more exciting than the *Come Close* project and sure enough it was. We actually had a film crew come and spend a week with us filming around the house as I went about my daily chores. They filmed me making tea and waking up the kids early in the morning for school (even though we filmed it in the middle of the afternoon. The kids just put their pyjamas on top of the day clothes. The team were great to work with and it gave us an insight into the amount of painstaking work that goes on into making a film. Even the tea-making sequence took two hours to film. I can't begin to tell you how many times that tea went back into the pot as they took shots from so many different angles.

When the programme was eventually shown it was well received and we did hear that some schools in the South of England took the video and used it as part of their religious education syllabus. Again we had to sign a contract regarding exclusive rights to the programme and we received £240 with which we were able to buy school uniforms for each of our children who were about to start at their new Comprehensive School. So you see, God again found a most unexpected way of providing for our needs and doing it in such an enjoyable way.

Over the years I have come to love Psalm 34 because so many of the verses have become real and personal in my life. Remember the washing machine story and the verse in the box 'The young lions lack and go hungry but those who trust in the Lord lack no good thing'? (Psalm 34:10) Then there was the grapefruit story and the verse 'Oh taste and see that the Lord is good' (Psalm 34:8). To those I would like to add 'My soul will make her boast in the Lord and the afflicted ones will hear and be made glad' (Psalm 34:2). More than anything else in life, I love to boast in the Lord confidently expecting that needy people will hear my enthusiastic heart of joy and themselves be made glad. Whilst I may be physically blind, my vision is to see the spiritual eyes of people opened to the glorious reality of God's love as revealed through His dear son the Lord Jesus Christ.

Whilst talking about the relevance that Psalm 34 has played in my life another story comes to mind. I was preaching one night in a Pentecostal Church in Birmingham on the verse in Psalm 34: 'I sought the Lord and He heard me and He delivered me from all of my fears'. As usual I was speaking fervently and with conviction, believing every word to be true. As I preached however God began to speak to me. This is an amazing thing in that while you are doing something else, the Lord can still engage with your spirit. The only thing was it was somewhat uncomfortable for me. I was preaching truth of course, but God was saying to me "Hypocrite".

I continued to preach with nobody I am sure having a clue what was going on inside me. I knew however that God was on my case again and that He would not let me go. Sometime later, I began to enquire of the Lord what He was talking to me about when He called me a hypocrite. Immediately God reminded me that although I was convinced that I had been delivered from all of my fears, there were in fact two things that he still wanted me to get victory over – water and the dentist.

I had pushed these two areas to the back of my mind and did not think they were important. God, however, desired for me to have no fear and He wanted me to live in victory over these two areas.

Victories and villains

My first victory took place at a new club that had been formed called 'Solihull Seals', and this was basically a group of people who were giving their time freely to take and teach disabled people to swim. I felt that God was on my case and providing an ideal opportunity for me.

I went along to the Tudor Grange swimming baths for several weeks on a Monday night and was introduced to a Dr McKenzie, then a local G.P. I immediately felt confident with him in a way that I never did with the teachers at school. I trusted him that he would not let me drown and within a few weeks he had me swimming and the 5 metres badge on my shorts for many years was one of my proudest possessions as yet another fear was met head on and overcome. At this time in my life an ear condition prevents me from going swimming, but at least I have overcome the fear and who knows what may happen in the future with the hand of God on the rudder of my life.

My fear of the dentist again went back to childhood and the full horror of my trip to the school dental clinic is told in the 'Fear' section of this book. As a result of those childhood experiences many people have ignored their teeth and refrained from visiting a Dentist for the rest of their lives. I may well have come into that category had not God got hold of my life. In effect what God, through the Holy Spirit, was saying to me was "How can you expect your

118

children to look after their teeth and go to the dentist every six months if you as their Dad does not set an example?" I understood that rationale and agreed with it totally. There is a Christian maxim which I wholeheartedly agree with that says "If Jesus is not Lord of all then He's not Lord at all". I had to do something about this area of inconsistency in my life and so I went ahead and booked an appointment with my local dentist.

Mr Fraser, my dentist, was a rather kind and gentleman who listened to my childhood experience of the school dentist with plenty of compassion, saying that he had heard the same story so many times from different people of my age group. On that first visit I was booked in to have one tooth out, a couple of fillings and a general clean up. I felt relaxed and confident and the sophisticated equipment and gentle nature of the dentist seemed light years away from the nightmare on Sheep Street. Since then I have gone every six months to see the dentist for many years and never even had to have a tooth out, just the very occasional filling. I have been able to set a good example in this area to Sylvia and the children and once again God has been glorified. I can once again say with confidence and this time hopefully with no interruptions from the good Lord, "I sought the Lord and He heard me and He delivered me from all my fears".

If I do find myself getting scared or facing a really nerve-racking situation then I find it helpful to think of Jesus suffering upon the Cross from the most incredible pain. Yet He did endure it and overcame without the need for painkillers, anaesthetic etc. As a Christian I believe that I am born again and that Jesus now lives in me through His Holy spirit. If that is true and that same Jesus who endured the pain upon the cross lives in me then I too can endure anything if I allow Him to live through me.

These were days when God was certainly on my case as it were. He had allowed me a few years to get established in the faith and to grow in my knowledge of Him. There were however certain anomalies in my life which He wanted me to get to grips with and so God the Holy Spirit started to get to work on me. Having already sorted me out with regard to my record collection and then the dentist, it was now time to turn His attentions to another big god in my life, namely Aston Villa.

My good friend Peter Jackson was working full time with an organisation by the name of the Torch Trust for the Blind and Torch used to hold fellowship meetings in Birmingham on Saturday afternoons at 3pm, lasting for about two hours in total. Of course for any self-respecting football fan (at least in those days pre Sky Television) 3pm on a Saturday afternoon was sacrosanct, being the time that most if not all games kicked off.

I had not missed an Aston Villa home game for many years and had no intention of doing so. Consequently whenever Peter invited me to attend Torch meetings, which was frequently, I would first of all consult the football fixture list to see if Aston Villa were playing at home or away. If they were at home on the day of the Torch meeting then I would make an excuse to the effect that I already had a prior engagement.

Even when Villa were playing away from home on the Saturday of the Torch meeting I would still take my transistor radio and have a sneaky listen to the score from time to time throughout the meeting. I must confess to feeling somewhat awkward about this clash of loyalties.

One night while sitting at home I received a phone call.

"Hello John, my name is David McCulloch and I am Pastor of the Church of the Nazarene in Small Heath, Birmingham".

David spoke in a soft, but strong Scottish accent and he was inviting me to speak at a coffee bar his church was running in their locality. He wanted me to tell my story of how I came to faith in Christ and of the difference he had made to my life. He said they usually attracted about 30 young people to the coffee bar.

"Yes of course David, I would be thrilled to come along" was my enthusiastic reply, "When do you meet?"

I was shocked and disappointed when David said that the coffee bar was held each Saturday afternoon between 3-5pm.

"Just one moment" I said as I sent Sylvia scurrying for the diary and the fixture list.

David gave me a date but it coincided with Villa being at home so I asked for another date and on the second occasion I managed to agree a date when Villa were playing away, but I was still upset that it was Saturday because that had always been my day for sport. By now of course I was sensing that God was pinning me down on the issue and I was starting to feel uncomfortable. Jesus was definitely my personal Saviour, but I could not say with absolute conviction that He was my Lord also.

On the original date that I should have been at the coffee bar, Villa I think were at home to Bristol City and I went to the game but can't say that I enjoyed it. I cannot remember the game or anything about it. What I can remember however is the terrible feeling of guilt. I should have been at the coffee bar, serving my God and though I had deceived the Pastor, the God who sees and knows all knew what was in my heart. There were split loyalties and on that day I made up my mind that when the season finished a few weeks later that was it for me and football. In those days I had a privileged seat at Villa Park in the press box where I was able to listen to a commentary on the headphones, which was being broadcast to local hospitals and the commentators were really shocked when I told them that I would not be going back. With God's help I kept to my word and for the next four seasons I never again went to Villa Park though I did still maintain a very close interest in the scores and performances via my radio. I felt relieved and happy that I could again say with conviction "Jesus is Lord of my life".

I refused a number of invitations to go back to Villa Park and some were even questioning if I was inferring that going to football matches was a sin. I said that it had become a sin for me because it was rivalling God for the most important place in my life. There came a time however when a friend, Brian Davis, rang me up to say that he had a spare ticket for an Aston Villa versus West Ham United game and was I interested in going with him. Initially I politely turned the offer down, but Sylvia had words with me saying;

"I feel that you should go to that game with Brian. The time together would be good for you both".

"But what if I get hooked again?" I protested.

Sylvia said, "I don't think you will, because God has done a work in your heart".

Somewhat nervously it has to be said, I got back in touch with Brian and accepted his offer. Thankfully he still had the tickets. We went to the game, had a great time together and Villa won 4-0, which of course made my day. What was even better was that when the next match came around I did not go and did not have any great desire to go either. I have since discovered that I can go to games or not as the case may be. I still love Aston Villa and follow them passionately. That is the way I am but I rarely go to the games these days.

I did have several years when I had a season ticket with my son Ian. I started to take him to Villa Park when he was 7 years of age and we have shared some magical times together as father and son. One little tradition that we developed was that on the way to the game we would stop off at our favourite fish and chip shop near to Villa Park in Manor road; the same fish and chip shop where I used to go many years before as a teenager with my friends Ronnie and Brian.

Ian and I would always have a 'Match Day Special' which consisted of fish, chips, jumbo sausage and optional curry sauce or mushy peas. Ian always had the curry but I declined because I did not fancy the idea of fingers smelling of curry for the rest of the afternoon. In all weathers we have stood outside that fish and chip shop enjoying our delicious pre match meal. We often joked saying that even if the match turned out to be lousy you could always rely on the 'Match Day Special' to be brilliant and excellent value at £1.60, which it was for many years.

Of course I have learned from this that if anything has a hold over my life and takes the place of Jesus Christ as number one then it has to go. Some people, like drug addicts or alcoholics for instance, find it better to cut the object of their addictions out of their life completely and I fully understand that especially in those cases.

There are other things however, like football in my case that can dominate our lives to the point where God is relegated to second or third place. God does not want to rob us of the enjoyment of such things but simply to help us to put everything in its right order. The Bible teaches that one of the evident fruits of the Holy Spirit ruling in our lives is that we will have self-control. We will know when to say yes and when to say no. Hopefully I have learned that lesson, though as life goes on, my experience is that there are always new challenges to face when it comes to walking by faith and listening to the Holy spirit as He seeks to lead me in the will of God the Father.

I will keep on coming back to this time and time again, but possibly the most exciting thing about being a Christian is to have the Holy Spirit, God himself, living on the inside. That's what happens when a person becomes a Christian and The Bible calls it 'being born again of incorruptible seed'. It truly is amazing and I only wish I along with millions of other believers were quiet and still often enough to hear the voice of God. Though He is so mighty, awesome and powerful, yet more often than not He speaks in a still small voice, and is gentle as a dove.

One such time was when I sensed that God was speaking to me about the need for some kind of pedestrian crossings outside Lode Heath School in Solihull. A few children had been knocked down and seriously injured over the years and it seemed like only a matter of time before someone was killed. On at least two occasions I felt a stirring on the inside that I should start a campaign to get some crossings, but I chose to ignore the thought, until one eventful day that is. It was about 3.15pm in the afternoon and I was just about to leave home to meet a friend in Solihull town centre when the phone rang. The call was of no great importance and only lasted about two minutes, however it was sufficient time for me to just miss my bus. My choice now was to wait 30 minutes for the next one and be late for my meeting or walk a little further to catch a bus on a different route. I chose the latter option and it was a good job I did (thank you Jesus for the phone call). Whilst I was striding out in the general direction of Lode Heath School, I was met by the anguished voice of a girl running breathlessly home from school.

"Mr Flanner" she shrieked, "one of the twins has been involved in an accident, she is lying on the road in Lode Lane".

The distraught girl was not able to give me any more clear information and so I hurried along the winding road as fast as my legs would carry me, occasionally breaking out into a trot and flailing my white stick around in front of me. Other children came along and confirmed that it was Allison who had been hit by a car and that an ambulance had just arrived.

I arrived at the scene to find that Allison had just been placed in the back of the ambulance and she was going to be taken to Birmingham's Heartlands hospital. She was conscious and though in a lot of pain she was able to give me a hug and between the tears talk to me a little. Outside of the main school gates it is a dual carriageway and though there were traffic lights about 100 yards up the road, most of the children who lived on the Damsonwood housing estate tended to come straight out of school, cross halfway and then wait on the small embankment in the middle of the road. Often there is a crowd of children jostling on the embankment as was the case on this particular day. Allison then

123

11 years of age, was pushed slightly in the back causing her to slip into the road into the path of an oncoming car. The car caught the handle of Allison's school bag and dragged her along the road for a short distance at a fair old speed however. The impact caused Allison to sufferer a broken ankle and a collapsed lung. I was so thankful that God had changed my schedule and arranged for me to be there to comfort Allison, to pray for her in the ambulance and to accompany her to hospital.

Ironically Sylvia was stuck in a traffic jam at the end of Lode Lane which had been caused by this accident. Sylvia was returning from visiting someone in the very hospital where her daughter was now being taken to. In the traffic jam that ensued Sylvia wound her car window down and enquired of a passer-by, "What has happened?"

"A child has been involved in an accident while coming out of school" came the reply.

Sylvia immediately began to pray using the gift of speaking in tongues that I spoke about earlier in the book, not knowing at that stage of course that it was one of her own children. As she got nearer home however she did ascertain that it was Allison who had been involved in the accident. On arriving home, Sylvia picked up Beverley and Sara and they then set off for the hospital to meet up with Allison and me.

Thankfully after a few months Allison had made a full physical recovery from her injuries though in truth it probably took a lot longer to overcome the emotional scars of what had happened. I would point out that on that particular day Allison was in a hurry to get home as we were taking delivery of a pet bird – a cute little yellow budgerigar who we named Chico. Yes that's right the very bird who later learned to bite the dots off my Braille Bible.

The accident involving our own daughter prompted me into action and I started a campaign to get crossings installed. I invited people to sign a petition getting in all over 200 signatures and I also secured a very convincing letter from Mr Evans, the Head Teacher from Lode Heath School at the time. I eventually submitted the application to the Solihull Council and was overjoyed when the news came through that permission had been granted for some pelican crossings to be installed right outside the school gates near to where Allison had sustained her injuries.

In my eyes now these are the 'Allison Crossings' and it got even better some years later when across the road from the school right by the crossings, planning permission was granted for a church to be built on the site of an old coach factory. Now the Allison Crossings not only guide children safely to and from school but they also guide people safely to the Renewal Christian Centre, which has a congregation of close on 2,000 people and is one of the fastest growing churches in the United Kingdom. I am so glad that I heard and obeyed the Holy Spirit and I only wish I had done it earlier, it may well have saved Allison, her Mum and a lot of other people a great deal of heartache.

My time at Torch

Having resolved the issue of who was really Lord of my life, Saturday afternoons were freed up for me and I was able to attend the meeting of the Birmingham Torch Fellowship. They were held monthly at 3pm on a Saturday afternoon in a purpose-built Social Services centre in the Edgbaston area of Birmingham. About 100 people would gather to sing traditional hymns, modern Gospel choruses, hear Bible readings, maybe listen to a soloist and hear a short presentation of the Gospel message, usually from a visiting speaker. The meeting all told would last for around 90 minutes and then we would all enjoy a sit down tea of sandwiches, cakes, jelly and trifle followed by tea or coffee.

These fellowship group meetings depended so much on volunteers from local churches, picking up the blind or partially sighted person by car from their home, taking them to the meeting and then taking them home afterwards. Some volunteers would stay for the meeting whilst others would go home or do shopping and then come back at the end of the meeting.

From a personal point of view I would say that I found the meetings to be somewhat old fashioned, however, what I cannot deny is that they were meeting a great need. Many of the folk who came along were not just blind, but often had other disabilities as well. They were often lonely people who would not go near a traditional church for a variety of reasons, so in that respect Torch Fellowship groups were meeting a very clear need both socially and spiritually.

The inspiration and driving force behind these fellowship groups, of which there were over 100 across the United Kingdom in the 1970s, was my good friend and inspiration, Peter Jackson. At one of the Birmingham Torch Fellowship meetings Peter began to talk to me about his conviction that there was a need for a Torch Fellowship group to be established in the area of Sutton Coldfield. Having sewed the seed thought in my mind, for the most part Peter was happy to leave it to the Holy Spirit to get to work on me, but Peter was never slow to remind me of his desire for a Sutton Coldfield Torch Fellowship whenever we met or spoke on the phone.

I was still working with Sylvia and others on the Wyrley Birch Housing Estate at the time and I had developed links with six or seven local churches. In those churches I knew of folk who did voluntary work for Torch and so I decided to call a meeting of all of those workers and anyone else who may be interested in seeing a Torch Fellowship group in Sutton Coldfield. I invited Peter Jackson along to share his vision for such a group and arising from that initial meeting about eight of us began to meet together for prayer meetings and to seek God for his guidance.

Eventually we put together a committee to get the project off the ground. We did some deputation meetings in churches around Sutton Coldfield to share the vision of what Torch and the fellowship groups were all about and stressed our need for further volunteers. After a lot of ground work the Sutton Coldfield Torch Fellowship group was launched and it ran for many years with attendances usually hovering around the 100 mark. A tremendous sense of fellowship was created and many new and lasting friendships were forged. It was a real thrill too of course to know that a considerable number of blind and partially sighted people came to know Jesus in those days and though they have now long since died, it is heartening to know that they are safe and present with the Lord. It was also great to be a part of so many local churches from different doctrinal persuasions, working together for the one cause.

I had a wonderful group of people working with me on the Torch Fellowship Group and the only reason I do not mention them by name is for the fact that I am sure to miss somebody out and I would not wish to cause offence in that way. Suffice to say that all involved in the work of Sutton Coldfield Torch Fellowship and also in supporting Sylvia and me on the housing estate will all have their rewards directly from the Lord Jesus Christ one day.

The Torch Trust for the Blind was growing rapidly at this stage, not just in the fellowship groups around the country, but also in the production of Christian literature in braille and audio form which was accessible to blind, partially sighted and deaf-blind people of all ages. The full and amazing story of the Torch Family can be read in an exciting autobiographical book written by the founders Ron and Stella Heath. As the trust grew in the 1970's it became clear that there was a real need for more folk with the necessary communication skills to be able to go around the country to make known what it was that Torch had to offer.

When I became aware of this need I did wonder to myself whether this was the kind of thing I should be looking at as a next step in ministry. Out of the blue I was then contacted by Peter, who asked me if I would prayerfully consider becoming his assistant, which would mainly mean me travelling to some of the fellowship groups around the UK to speak at their meetings and to meet with and encourage the workers on the local committees. In addition I would be expected to undertake some deputation meetings in local churches to talk about the work, set forth the vision and stress that there was always a need for more volunteers. Torch also needed people who would agree to put themselves forward to be voice tested, because there was (and still is) a great need for people to read books on to tape.

I was starting to feel that Sylvia and I had given so much of ourselves over a five year period working on the housing estate that in a way we and the kids needed something fresh. For several months Sylvia and I were very hesitant about what we should do and after these years of not having a regular income, working for Torch offered us a steady salary which made it very appealing. A big downside for us would that it would mean leaving our beloved council house that had come to mean so much to us.

I honestly cannot remember what eventually clinched it for us but we came to a point where we were able to say to Peter that I was willing to come on board as a member of staff with Torch and work alongside him in the outreach work across the country. The work on the housing estate was handed over to the church of which we were members at the time.

Sylvia drove me over to Torch House at Hallaton Hall, appreciating and taking in the lovely Leicestershire countryside as we travelled. Our three daughters, Beverley, Sara and Allison all came along too and revelled in the vastness of Torch House and in its superbly manicured lawns and gardens. I met with Ron, Stella and Peter plus a few other Committee members. A job description was drawn up, a salary agreed and a few encouraging prayers said over me, including one that as a family we would find somewhere to live in the Market Harborough locality very quickly. Peter Jackson and his wife Margaret had already made the move from Birmingham and were buying a nice house on a new housing development called Farndon Fields in Market Harborough itself.

I quickly discovered that I would need to have a diary with me at all times when attending Torch House. There were always piles of letters from churches and social service groups, requesting visits from Torch staff in order to explain about the work. So it was that ministry and deputation tours were put together on a monthly basis and it was my very first trip without Peter being there to support me that led to something truly astonishing taking place.

There were three of us on the Torch outreach team that weekend in Sussex. We helped out with leading the Eastbourne Torch Fellowship group on the Saturday afternoon and then did a deputation meeting on the Saturday night in a small Gospel Hall. On the Sunday morning we were still in Eastbourne attending a Baptist Church at which I was the guest preacher. Little did I know at the time, but my words were to have quite an impact on a particular lady sitting in the congregation that morning. On returning home from Eastbourne, Sylvia and I began to make plans for our family holiday in the summer of 1976. We had booked a caravan for ourselves and our three daughters together with a family friend by the name of Celia (who I made mention of earlier as she was part of the lunchtime fellowship meeting at the Inland Revenue) and we were attending a Christian event called the Caple Bible Week, which was situated in a beautiful part of the country in the county of Surrey.

Celia, a single lady, had been someone who had helped us in our work on the Estate and had been a tremendous prayer support to us. We wanted to bless her with a holiday, include her as part of our family and allow her to serve us with baby-sitting duties on one or two nights so that Sylvia and I could get to some of the meetings together. There were always specialist meetings in huge marquees for children and young people. For adults there were meetings in the big top morning, afternoon and evening, each one lasting around two hours. With great music, great speakers, great weather and a babysitter we were guaranteed a wonderful week. What we were certainly not guaranteed were the events of the Wednesday afternoon.

128

Sylvia and I had already decided that we were going to take one day off from the Bible Week and whisk the children off to the beach in Brighton which was about an hour's drive away. We had a lovely day arriving back at our caravan at about 4pm. As Sylvia was about to insert her key into the caravan door she saw a note pinned to the door itself. The note simply requested that we telephone a number in Godstone. We were puzzled as we did not know where Godstone was and neither did Celia.

We were obviously intrigued and half dreaded ringing the number in case our lovely week was going to be marred with some bad news. Sylvia stayed behind at the caravan to start getting the tea ready whilst I went off to the phones with Celia. I hesitantly dialled the numbers as Celia read them out to me.

A well-spoken lady answered the phone with a warm "Hello Mrs Watts speaking".

Not recognising the name, I simply said, "My name is John Flanner, I am attending the Caple Bible Week with my family and I have had a message to ring your number".

With that Mrs Watts relaxed and said "Oh yes I drove up to the site this afternoon, but you had obviously gone out for the day, so I pinned the note on your caravan door." Mrs Watts continued enthusiastically, "John, I was in Eastbourne on holiday last week and I attended the Baptist Church where you were preaching on the Sunday. I am a prayer and financial partner with the Torch Trust and I felt that God spoke to me about your need of a house".

Needless to say I was riveted to her every word by now as she continued, "I have been up to Market Harborough this week and across the road from Peter and Margaret Jackson is a brand new Georgian style three bedroom house which is still empty. I hope you don't mind John, but I actually put a deposit on it and reserved it for you".

This was turning into one of my more amazing telephone calls and I was thinking, "Does this lady know I can't afford to buy a house?" However it soon transpired that this was not in Mrs Watts' thinking at all. "I recently came into some money John and I want to buy the house for you so that you can move from Birmingham and be more fully involved in the work of Torch, so is that okay?"

I was stunned, of course I was and said "Yes, that's amazing".

Mrs Watts picked up the conversation again by informing me that there was a very tight time limit on this as the houses were in great demand so could we go over to Market Harborough the following week to have a look at the house and let her know as a matter of priority whether we wanted the house or not as she needed to make arrangements for the money to be released.

Celia had been listening to my end of this telephone conversation and had gathered that something unusual was happening. She heard me thank Mrs Watts so many times before closing the conversation with a series of "thank yous" for I just did not know what else to say. I did discover from my conversation that Godstone was only a few miles down the road from where we were camped and that Mrs Watts' son Phil, with whom we were to become good friends, also worked at Torch and was resident with other staff at Hallaton.

When I got back to the caravan and tried to relay this story to Sylvia it sent her, quite understandably I think, into a bit of a spin. We were excited as we talked this over and having already visited Peter and Margaret Jackson in their new home, Sylvia already knew that Watson Avenue was a really lovely road and that the house in question was very nice indeed. In fact on our visit to the Jacksons, Sylvia had gone across the road with Margaret and looked through the windows with Margaret saying, "Wouldn't it be great if you could afford to buy that?"

The Bible week over and having had a feast of spiritual food we arrived home looking forward to our trip to Market Harborough to visit what looked as if it was going to be our new home. Time and time again we marvelled that anyone should be generous enough to want to buy us our own house but we concluded that however was just a small sample of God's immeasurable love to us. The day duly came and we made our way over to Market Harborough to look at the house and as we went around it was hard to imagine that this was going to shortly become home for us. As the Agent showed us around, Sylvia was busily working out in her mind where all the furniture would go, whilst I took the opportunity to go across the road to the Jacksons' house and ring Mrs Watts to confirm our acceptance of her kind offer.

"Wonderful" she said, "I will immediately set the wheels in motion and get the relevant paperwork to you as quickly as possible".

Back at our home in Birmingham we began to make plans for our first ever move from the city of our birth. In addition it was still hard to comprehend that through someone else's incredible generosity we were shortly going to be the owners of our own house and mortgage-free too, which was even more amazing. Those thoughts however turned out to be a bit premature though as the days turned into weeks while we waited in vain for the promised paperwork to arrive. Finally our curiosity at the seemingly long delay got the better of us and I decided that I would have to ring Mrs Watts to find out if everything was still okay.

As she answered the phone I said, "Please forgive my impatience, but we are very excited and wondered what the latest position is".

Mrs Watts, who we now knew as Vivian, was clearly embarrassed as she explained "I'm really sorry John, but there's been a serious hiccup in proceedings. There has been a legal problem in regard to some money I have been bequeathed and as a result I cannot buy the house for you. I'm so terribly sorry."

I gulped with disbelief and disappointment as Vivian continued to explain.

"I can buy the house in my name and then invite you to move in and just be responsible for paying the rates".

We were left having to make a decision and though it was a far cry from owning our own house, eventually, we did come to the conclusion that it was still an answer to prayer. We had been praying for accommodation in Market Harborough and God was providing us with a beautiful home in an ideal location. Sure we were disappointed, but we had to overcome that and move forward in good faith that God was in it.

Things began to move quickly now and having sorted out any embarrassment with Vivian, who was clearly even more upset by events than ourselves, we were soon safely ensconced in our new home. It was so good having our friends Peter and Margaret across the road and we got together regularly for meals, shopping trips and games of scrabble. Our three little girls, Beverley, Sara and Allison all started at Farndon Fields School where they settled in really well. We had quite a few visitors from Birmingham coming to see us and Sylvia loved to take them out to visit the nearby Foxton locks for a gentle walk along the canal towpath. It was so tranquil living close to the countryside, far removed from the hustle and bustle of the big city.

On the work front I was beginning to develop a schedule of trips across the UK to undertake a mixture of deputation and preaching appointments. I really did enjoy the travelling, meeting new people and especially having so many wonderful opportunities to share my faith. Paradoxically, however, I hated being away from home and I missed Sylvia and the children so much.

One of my first trips after moving to Market Harborough was a 10 day tour of the West Country, taking in churches in Somerset, Devon and Cornwall. In the months that followed I had some very enjoyable ministry trips across the country visiting many Torch Fellowship groups in England, Scotland, Wales and Northern Ireland. I worked hard at being friendly and getting on with people at all times, but there were several occasions where my boldness or spontaneity was frowned upon, and as a result I had a lingering suspicion with certain people that if I said the slightest thing wrong I would be pulled in line.

My favourite times were when I was travelling with Peter Jackson. We got on so well and he was a wonderful encouragement to me. I gained so much from seeing him at work talking with people. Whether it was in a situation with Social Services or meeting with folk in Church, Peter was always courteous, respectful and never afraid to call on his sharp wit to lighten an atmosphere or defuse a potentially difficult situation.

Back home the kids had settled well into school and Sylvia was having some good times with Margaret, discovering the new shopping opportunities in Market Harborough, Leicester and Kettering as well as driving into Torch House and helping out there from time to time with a variety of odd jobs. As the months went by however a few situations began to concern me. Although we made some good friends at Torch and the ministry they have is a wonderful one, somehow I never felt as though I truly belonged to the Torch family in the way that many others did. One of the regular meetings that I had to attend at Torch House was the Diary Meeting when we prayed over invitations that were coming in for deputation and preaching work. On the one hand I felt quite good about seeing my diary getting booked up for two years ahead, it was nice to be wanted as it were, but what I was not happy with however was the amount of time I was going to be spending away from Sylvia and the children, especially at weekends. There came a point when I realised that Sylvia was lonely and it was extremely hard work having three young children around with Dad away so often.

As I travelled around the country and stayed in the homes of many Christians, it was very interesting the way people opened up their hearts to me in a way that maybe they would not have to their local Minister. I became seriously concerned about the number of Christian marriages that were on the rocks as it were and one night I felt God say to me "Yes and yours will go the same way unless you give attention to it".

I tried to negotiate a reduction in the amount of time that I was spending away from home, but I was told that I was called to the work as an evangelist and that being away from home was one of the prices that an evangelist had to pay. In the end I just said "Well I am not prepared to pay it" and shortly afterwards I wrote out my resignation letter which was accepted without a fuss and my slightly turbulent years as a full time worker with Torch came to an end.

Then there was the matter of the house that was ours only as long as we worked for Torch, however Vivian was very gracious and did not put any pressure on us to move. In fairness, Torch were very good for even though my leaving must have been a disappointment to them, they agreed to keep on paying me a nominal sum until we had found the way forward for our lives. This was one of the most difficult times of my life to date. Although I had sought to do what was right and be obedient to God, I was nevertheless overwhelmed with a sense of failure, and felt like I was a big disappointment to the folk at Torch, to Peter and Margaret who had given us so much support and after making the decision to move from Birmingham, we were now in a strange town, with no job and no local church affiliation, so where do we go from here?

Starting again

One of our priorities after I left Torch Trust was to find a church where we could worship as a family and start to feel at home. There were some really nice Christian people that we had got to know in Market Harborough, but they all seemed to come from fairly traditional and quite staid backgrounds.

With the experience I had gained from visiting many churches of various doctrinal persuasions around the country and also through reading magazines as well as the Caple Bible Week, I had become aware of a new style of church that was being raised up by God across the country and indeed across the world. These were places where the praise and worship was lively, often spontaneous and containing many new songs mixed in with the traditional hymns.

In these newer churches there was also a strong emphasis on loving one another, helping each other in practical ways and sharing God's love out into the community. Somehow this fresh approach was appealing to us and it seemed very Biblical when we looked at the New Testament part of the Bible.

Leicester Christian Fellowship was about 15 miles away, but as the cliché says, 'A Church alive is worth the drive'. Another departure from the norm with regard to Leicester Christian Fellowship was that they met for worship at 3pm on a Sunday afternoon and we'd certainly not known that before. After a few weeks of attending we were enjoying being there without ever really feeling totally at home.

One Saturday Leicester Christian Fellowship were holding a leaders day and this was open to other church leaders from their particular group of churches from around the Midlands area. I was pleasantly surprised when one of the Elders of Leicester Christian Fellowship invited me to attend the day and he even arranged transport for me. I was even more shocked on arriving for the first session to find that two of my friends from Solihull Christian Fellowship were there; Steve Wood (who was actually doing the teaching for the day) and my old friend and former boss Bryan Pullinger.

I enjoyed the day enormously and it was a great opportunity to be refreshed in a spiritual sense. During the break times, especially over lunch, I was able to talk with Bryan about how I had come to leave Torch and how I needed to find work. Most important of all at this time was to rediscover God's will for us as a family. Bryan agreed to go back and to get the folk at Solihull Christian Fellowship to pray for us.

A week or two later Sylvia received a phone call from Bryan's wife, Jenny who said that if we were available she and Bryan wanted to drive over to see us. They duly arrived suitably loaded up with bags of groceries and a gift of £50, which all came with love from the church folk. It was much needed and a great relief I can assure you. After a gentle stroll around the wooded lanes we arrived back at our house in Watson Avenue ready for Bryan and Jenny's departure back to Solihull. I will never forget Jenny's parting words, "Lovely house, but don't stay here if God is not in it".

"But where can we go?" queried Sylvia.

"Why not Solihull?" Jenny said, "After all God is able to provide".

Well He truly is able to provide and the way in which God got us out of Market Harborough is every bit as remarkable, if not more so, than how He got us there in the first place. I had signed on at the Job Centre in Market Harborough and began looking for work. I have always known that God had called me to work for Him ever since He said "Launch out into the deep" in relation to working on the housing estate back in Birmingham. I sensed that my life would be characterised by me becoming a man of faith who would be continually launching out into the deep.

At this particular point in my life I felt it was time to turn to the only employable skill that I knew I had and that was being an audio typist. Nothing had materialised when out of the blue came yet another telephone call. It was again, my friend and former work colleague, Bryan Pullinger.

"John" he said, "The Inland Revenue are going to be opening up a new office in Solihull in a few months' time and I do know that they will be recruiting audio typists, so if you are interested I will have an application form sent to you".

I did say yes to Bryan, but I think, with not a great deal of enthusiasm. We had not been in Market Harborough a year and the thought of moving again was to me not a realistic prospect. I did not want to put Sylvia and the children through that ordeal, especially as the kids had settled into a nice country school. The other thing was that it would have seemed like admitting failure and my pride did not like that. I continued looking for work in Market Harborough, but without any semblance of success.

Then came a most surprising letter in the post. It was from the Inland Revenue and stated that I was being offered a job as an audio typist at the new Special Office which was being opened at Chadwick House in Solihull in the autumn of 1977. On the strength of my previous service I would be taken on without having to go through an interview procedure, although I would have to complete the application form. I think you will agree this was a pretty interesting development and in terms of seeking God's will for the next stage of our life, one not to be discarded lightly. I telephoned the personnel officer whose name was on the letter and had a chat about the job and also explained my situation in terms of where I was living and that I would have to find somewhere to live in the vicinity of the new office.

The lady was most agreeable understanding and even agreed to hold the job open for a month or two to enable us to move to the area. Sylvia and I chatted further with Bryan and Jenny on the phone, in particular about finding somewhere to live. Bryan agreed to check out the situation with regard to Council housing in Solihull and also write to a number of Housing Associations for us. They also invited us over to Solihull to have lunch with them on Sunday and visit their church.

The Solihull Christian Fellowship started life as house group and when we visited there were about 50 people, mainly young and middle aged, meeting in a room at what was then the Solihull Civic Hall. What struck us was the warmth and friendliness of the welcome we and other visitors were given, I have never been hugged so tightly by so many people in such a short time in all my life.

The other thing was that the music and singing were really joyful, exuberant and demonstrative with hands raised and plenty of dancing going on. It was great fun and we really enjoyed it; so too did the children which was very important to us in view of the changes that had been taking place in their lives too.

After enjoying dinner with the Pullingers' we headed off back to Market Harborough, with Sylvia commenting, "I really felt at home in that church".

I did too in fact, but I think my confidence had taken a battering, because I still could not see how we would get to move to Solihull, or anywhere near it for that matter. We did however decide to continue going to Solihull each Sunday in time for the morning service, all the time praying and hoping that something would turn up from an accommodation perspective. Bryan had worked tirelessly for several weeks contacting Solihull Housing Department and also writing to numerous Housing Associations, but all to no avail. I was extremely grateful that the Inland Revenue were still keeping an audio typing job open for me, but for how long I wondered.

The following Sunday after yet another inspiring meeting, car loads of people left Solihull Christian fellowship making for Dorridge Park. We were happy to follow another family as Sylvia was not too sure where we were going. It was a lovely late summer's afternoon, ideal for a picnic, games of cricket and rounders etc. We sat around on the grass in family groups and all in all it was a very pleasant scene. There were lots of children of all ages too so Beverley, Sara and Allison had some great fun with their newly found friends.

By about 3pm however, the clear blue skies had given way to cloud and a few spots of rain and in keeping with a few other families, we decided it was time to pack up and make our way back down the M6 in the direction of home. We were almost back at the car when we became aware that we were being called by a couple who were running after us. Somewhat out of breath, they eventually arrived at our car and I think, by way of making initial conversation asked if we were going home at that moment. We said that it had got a bit chilly and as we had a fairly lengthy drive ahead of us just thought we would make tracks.

"Before you go" the gentleman said, "there's something we need to tell you. For some time now we have been aware of your need of somewhere to live and we have been praying about it".

My mind was already going back to Mrs Watts and a feeling of deja vu swept over me. The lady picked up the story as she said, "We have seen your commitment in coming all this way week after week and as we have recently come into some money we thought we would like to help you buy a house, so we would like you to receive this cheque as a gift with our love. There is a modern housing estate in Solihull called Damsonwood and there are some nice family homes up there, near to schools and shops, so if you are not in too much of a hurry why don't we take you for a look around?"

At this point I know that Sylvia shed a few tears and I was trying hard not to shake with emotion as our three little girls sat in the car, probably wondering what Mummy and Daddy were up to. Having recovered our composure only slightly we got in the car to follow this benevolent couple with me still clutching the envelope with the mysterious cheque still hidden from view. I opened the

137

envelope and showed Sylvia the cheque and she gasped loudly when she saw the amount and had we not been following someone I know she would have pulled over in order to have a good cry. She could hardly get her words out as she said, "My God, it's for thirteen thousand pounds".

This time we all gasped including the children as I put them in the picture as to what was happening to us on this amazing Sunday afternoon. Even though they were only five years of age, they burst into squeals of delight. Soon we were pulling into what looked as if it could be the estate in question with loads of modern looking flats, maisonettes and a variety of different styled houses.

We drove around the estate following our benevolent couple and they slowed right down each time we saw a "For Sale" board outside a house. We actually got out and looked in through the windows of some of them. Our friends (who we later discovered were the same people who bought that washing machine for us four years earlier) knew the Damsonwood estate very well as they had other friends living there, knew exactly what kind of house they were looking for and which would suit us down to the ground.

We eventually pulled up outside one and it certainly had a feel good factor about it for all of us, but in order to view we had to ring the Estate Agent. The following day we made that call and fixed up a time for viewing. This indeed was the house from where the wallpaper story told earlier in the book emanated from and as you know from that, we did in fact go ahead and purchase the house. Subsequently we said our goodbyes to Market Harborough and to our great friends Peter and Margaret Jackson and left for Solihull just 15 months after leaving Birmingham in the first place. In fact we left Watson Avenue on the Friday and I commenced my new job as an audio typist with Inland Revenue Special Office the following Monday.

This was the beginning of a very settled and happy period of our lives. Church life was great, the work was extremely interesting and the children were a joy to us as they grew up in this most pleasing of environments. Outside our three bedroom end town house we had a nice garden with a cherry tree in the middle of it where our daughters would often sit and play with their friends. Beyond our garden was a lovely green area with trees where again the many little children living around the green could play in safety. I suppose you know the old saying 'New house, new baby'? Well it's true, or at least it was in our case. Settled into our new home, church and work we discovered that Sylvia was pregnant. After a reasonably trouble-free pregnancy (you can tell it's a man writing can't you!) Sylvia gave birth to our one and only son. Ian Paul was born on 5 September 1978 in Solihull Hospital.

A single lady from church made herself available for baby-sitting whenever I wanted to go hospital visiting to see Sylvia and my new son. Joy was a wonderful provision of God for us during those years because every time the children needed new shoes she made herself available to buy them for us, which was no small expense even in those days. Ever since getting married, wherever we had lived and gone to church, God had always seen to it that we had some truly wonderful, faithful friends and our lives had been enriched because of that. Now it was about to happen again.

Gordon and Julia Coleman really were and still are quite a remarkable couple. Their capacity to love people seems to know no bounds. I first got to know them, when Julia invited us to their house for Boxing Day celebrations on our first Christmas in Solihull. They had met and married in London. Julia was a nurse and Gordon had trained as a Doctor in general practice. They had moved to Solihull not long before us and like us had settled into life at the Solihull Christian Fellowship. In fact it was on that Boxing Day that Gordon had done a pregnancy test on Sylvia and was able to confirm that she was in fact expecting. When we first met Gordon and Julia they had two small children, Jonathan and Mark but two others soon followed in Timothy and Ruth. We got on brilliantly as two families and as the children were growing up we had some wonderful holidays together with so many laughs along the way. Gordon and I had this terrific banter going between us and we could bounce off each other in a jocular kind of a way so easily, in the same way that Morecambe and Wise used to do all those years ago.

Gordon used to often get his leg pulled because you never saw him without a shirt and tie, as befits a man of stature like a Doctor you might say. We used to wonder if Gordon even slept in his shirt and tie. Being the man he is he would often play up to this role and on holiday once, we were on a beach near Towyn in Wales and Gordon was getting changed into his swimwear under a huge beach towel. Suddenly Gordon began to make the sound of a trumpet fanfare and emerged in just his swimming trunks and his tie around his neck. He then took off dragging me with him running along the beach with his tie trailing in the wind, to the great amusement of our wives and children, not to mention the countless holidaymakers looking on in astonishment.

Gordon was actually born in Iran, one of four sons born to John and Audrey Coleman who were medical missionaries in Iran. This could explain in part why it is that Gordon hardly ever buys anything without bartering for it first. Anyway the family were forced into the International spotlight back in 1981 when Gordon's parents were taken hostage in Iran on suspicion of spying. They were in captivity for six months until the Archbishop of Canterbury's Special Envoy; Terry Waite flew out to Iran and negotiated their release. It turned out to be a wonderful story because John and Audrey, who had warm affection for the Iranian people, gained the respect of their captors and with a number of them became good friends, almost seeing them as their own sons. It was such a privilege to be close to the family in those days to witness the dignity with which they handled the whole episode. Truly this was Christian love and character being lived out before our very eyes.

These were relatively quiet years for us with me having a settled job that I enjoyed and with us being happy members of Solihull Christian Fellowship. I still had a passion for sharing the good news about Jesus and on one occasion I managed to persuade our church Elders to agree to a mission in our local pub, The Golden Acres. I had heard that my good friend from Torch, Peter Jackson was in town and I had an idea to use him for an outreach event in our local pub. I had chatted with the pub landlord saying that I had a blind friend who was a professional pianist and could I invite him along as a guest to the pub to play a medley of old favourites and incorporate into that some Gospel tunes.

The manager thought it was a great idea and so too did the Elders of our church. The evening went well with more than the usual number of people turning up on a Monday and Tuesday night to hear Peter playing and sharing about the love of God between each medley. A couple of months later we had an American drama group visiting local churches and I was able to get them into the pub as well so that they could present the Christian message through their very well performed drama sketches.

I was also enjoying working with Rev Michael Blood on BBC Radio WM. I was on once a month to review and chat about the latest Christian music releases with presenter Nicky Steele, a local disc jockey and fellow Aston Villa supporter, who is sadly no longer with us after his untimely death a few years ago.

Apart from our football team Nicky and I also shared a common enjoyment of soul music. These sequences would be edited and then go out as a segment in Michael's Sunday morning religious programme, then called *A Word in Advance*, because when it began as a much shorter programme, the main feature would be a sermon preview. Over the years that I took part in the programme a number of recordings and artists made an impact, but none more so than *Love Song for No 2* by a Canadian duo by the name of Mickey and Bekki. I played the title track, which had a kind of Carpenters feel to it, giving it a big build up and calling all married couples to gather around their radios and listen to the words, because this was just for them. Of course I had no idea of the impact it was going to have, especially in one couple's relationship. Part of the song lyric is as follows:

I'll sing you a love song that came to my mind / It's not a typical love song because it's one of mine

Now when I say I love you, you know that it's true / Even though you're number two.

For Jesus is number one in my life / So second place will have to do for you

But I'm counting on spending the rest of my life in love with the two of you."

There are a couple of other verses too, but that is the gist of what is a very lovely song. In the week following the show Michael received a letter from a teacher who said that he had to write to say that the song *Love Song for No. 2* had been used by God to save his marriage. He told how he and his wife had had a blazing row that Sunday morning and he stormed out of the house, having packed his case, fully intending never to return. As far as he was concerned it was all over. However, as he was driving away in his car, he heard me invite all married couples to gather around their radios and listen to the words. In his anger he pulled the car over to the side, parked up and listened. God spoke to him through the song and he turned the car round went home and made things up with his wife.

Such is the power of music to be able to speak to and inspire people and if God is working through the music then it is an incredibly powerful means of communication, which reaches right into the spirit of men and women in a way that the spoken word does not seem able to do. An old Bible story tells of how King Saul when he was deeply troubled in his soul, sent for the shepherd boy

David to come and play the harp for him. As David played Saul's troubled mind was eased. That is the way I would like to use music, to bring love, peace and joy into people's lives.

My job as an audio typist in the Inland Revenue Special Office in Solihull was going well, the work was interesting and I worked for a really nice group of investigative tax Inspectors, which I know may well surprise you. It was at the time one of only four offices of its kind in the country and we worked together like a tight knit family unit. It helped me considerably that all of the Inspectors that I typed for were very keen on sport, especially football. I really had some good times there at Chadwick House and was even able to start a Christian Fellowship meeting once a week in the building for folk who wanted to meet for prayer, Bible study and mutual encouragement. We never had great numbers, but we did develop some quality friendships and were able to support each other through some difficult times. Through all of this, however, I could not shake off the deep conviction that my primary aim in life was to serve my God in a full time ministry capacity. After all it was He who had called me years earlier when on the Wyrley Birch Housing Estate to 'Launch out into the deep'. I have since come to realise that that was not a one off call to that housing estate, but it is about the whole of life.

On several occasions I spoke to my Elders at Solihull Christian Fellowship about this and eventually after I had been back at the Inland Revenue for four years it was agreed that I should resign my typing job in order to work full time for Solihull Christian Fellowship in a paid capacity. I was involved with leading one of the church house groups, being available for outreach and counselling work within the church and also taking up opportunities to speak in school assemblies and Religious Education classes. I was also able to continue responding to preaching invitations, get more involved with local radio and of course have more time to study the Bible and pray. That time working as an employee of the Solihull Christian Fellowship was financially the most comfortable time of my life because they really looked after me. In that regard I was very grateful to one of the leaders in the church at the time, a guy called Jonathan Wallis (son of the late Christian author and teacher Arthur Wallis) who argued that people should be paid not according to their needs but according to their worth. It was lovely one month, therefore, to get a most generous pay rise.

142

All of that said, however, there was still something which was not quite right. There was something missing. I did not feel that I was giving the church value for money and I was not feeling fulfilled spiritually. Alan Cameron, one of our Elders at the time and a dear friend, said I reminded him of a cricketer swinging his bat and not making connection with the ball. That was a pretty accurate analogy. I carried on for a while afterwards swinging my proverbial bat as lustily as ever, until events took a surprising and to many of us, a devastating twist. I had been made aware that things had become a little tense in the leadership of the church. It was all to do with the direction the church was going in and our Eldership of eight fine Christian men were finding it difficult to reach agreement on a number of issues. Following one momentous church meeting it transpired that four of the Elders were going to continue to lead the Solihull Christian Fellowship whilst the other four would seek God as to the way forward for them and their families. The problem with this arrangement was that these guys were our friends and it was one of the hardest things Sylvia and I have ever had to do, to choose which way to go.

In the end, rightly or wrongly, we did what we have always done and followed our hearts. The result was that along with about 20 others we decided to leave Solihull Christian Fellowship and many of our dear friends, including Bryan and Jenny Pullinger, Alan and Heather Cameron, and Gordon and Julia Coleman with whom we had enjoyed such wonderful times. Not to be sniffed at also was the fact that we left behind that generous salary that the church had honoured me with. All I can say is that in everything, even when it has been perceived to be a mistake, we have always tried to follow the leading of the Holy Spirit and to please God by our actions. I think it was at this time that I first discovered a verse in the Bible that has come to mean so much to me;

"Blessed are those who have set their hearts on pilgrimage, whose trust is in the Lord." (Psalm 84:5)

After a bit of a cooling off period when a number of us chilled out and did not attend church for a few weeks we were eventually drawn back together with a need for fellowship, to praise and worship God and to hear from God together about the way forward. It did eventually form into a new church, initially called New Covenant Church, then New Life Church and finally, at this moment in time anyway, The King's Church. Apart from its early days, however, we were not destined to be part of this new venture, because we were about to launch out once again.

Launching into the deep

It had been an interesting nine years in Solihull during which time we had seen the birth of Ian our one and only son and the growth of our three girls into teenagers. We had also been the subject of two television programmes for Central Television, conducted a campaign to get pelican crossings installed outside the school where Allison got knocked over and set up the Aston Villa Christian Supporters Association. I had also successfully initiated Ian into being an Aston Villa supporter and over the years we have enjoyed (and endured) some memorable times together at Villa Park and around the country at other grounds too. Most important of all, however, we have had many quality times together as father and son and that to me is priceless and irreplaceable. Indeed I would say that any time I have spent alone with any of my children has been precious as too is that spent with my wife.

It was one of those precious alone times with one of my daughters, which indirectly led to our next major change of direction. Sara (one of the twins) now aged 13 accompanied me on a three day trip to London. I was going to attend a Christian conference in Kensington on behalf of the breakaway group from Solihull Christian Fellowship. There was a man preaching at the conference from the USA by the name of Jerry Savelle (unknown to me at the time but destined to become one of my favourite preachers) and it was felt that he would have something to say which would be relevant to the way forward for us as a group. Jerry was from what is known as the *'Word of Faith'* camp in terms of his theology and that was certainly an emphasis that was coming into the UK Church at the time. In fact I found what he had to say to be balanced and inspiring. Then and since I have found Jerry Savelle to be a man of integrity, fully conversant with the British way of thinking, which cannot be said for all foreign preachers.

While we were in London Sara and I stayed with some good friends. Harry and Joyce Hughes became known to me when I was working with Torch and I met them first at the Millmead Centre in Guildford. Harry was drawn to me because of my love for football. Not surprisingly really because Harry himself was an ex professional footballer, playing many times for and captaining Chelsea in the 1950s. Harry had become a Christian through the ministry of my good friend Peter Jackson a few years earlier and he had also had the distinction of being baptised by total immersion in the River Jordan whilst on a pilgrimage there. Harry was great fun to be around and handsome too and that is probably why Sara volunteered to come on this trip with me. All the kids loved Uncle Harry as they called him.

When Sara and I arrived in London we had trouble at the tube station because she got through the ticket barrier first whilst I was stuck on the other side trying to find where I had to insert my ticket. For some reason Sara got an attack of the giggles and could not get her words out to give me instructions as to where to put it and the more I struggled the more she laughed. It sounds cruel, but it was one of those moments when you have to be there to really appreciate the funny side of a simple situation. We then went from there and asked a newspaper seller if he could tell us the way to Kensington.

He startled us by saying, "Which one?"

We did not know there was more than one and this started Sara laughing all over again. "Is there more than one Kensington?" she said.

"Yes" said the man, "there's South Kensington and there's Kensington High Street, so which one do you want?"

Sara and I looked at each other and we decided to go for Kensington High Street. Thankfully it turned out to be the right one. Before going to Harry and Joyce's house we decided that as it was getting late we would be too late to expect Joyce to cook us a meal so we went to McDonalds. I was famished and went for a full meal, whilst Sara just went for a drink and chicken nuggets. She made the right choice because when we arrived at our destination, as soon as Joyce opened the door you could smell the aroma of a cooked meal. Harry and Joyce made us feel completely at home though as Sara and the others tucked into their roast dinner there were a few wry comments made about my apparent lack of appetite. Sara did not miss the opportunity to wind me up a little more either when our hosts disappeared into the kitchen to get the apple pie and custard. It sure was a struggle for me, but I made it in the end. I know it would have been simpler to have just admitted that we had been to McDonalds, but typical of me, I did not want to hurt Joyce's feelings.

During the conference in London and whilst the subject of my visit Jerry Savelle, was very good, it was somebody else who actually caught my attention for a completely different reason. Rev Dr Michael McCann, as he was introduced, was a very inspiring preacher, hailing from the American State of Wisconsin. I had never previously heard of him, but I was enraptured by his testimony of how God had brought him from his job as Dean of Students as the Christ for the Nations Bible Institute in Dallas, Texas to establish a similar Bible training centre in Cornwall, England.

Dr. McCann said that it was his vision to raise up men and women of passion and equip them with the necessary gifts to go out as mighty evangelists across the Continent of Europe and further afield to spread the gospel of the Lord Jesus Christ. I am the first to admit that up to that point I had been against the idea of Bible College, I suppose anything to do with school turned me off because of my negative experiences as a child. I don't think I had any particularly nasty experiences during my schooldays, but I could not wait to leave and get out into the real world. When it came to the matter of learning I always felt that I wasn't very good at it. Certainly taking exams turned me into a nervous wreck and from what I knew about Bible Colleges, they too seemed very academic.

What Dr. McCann seemed to be conveying, however, was that the college he ran in Cornwall was for anyone who had a call from God to full time ministry and desired to be better equipped with a knowledge of God's word, thus going out with a greater confidence to do His will. I was arouse and interested. I was also intrigued by the fact that I had recently been given some live worship tapes which were recorded at Christ for the Nations Institute in Dallas. Now here I was in London and through Michael McCann I was hearing about it again. On returning to Solihull I duly reported back to Steve Wood and the other folk in the group what I had gained from the conference as well as making available the tapes of the messages I had brought back with me. Personally, however, I could not shake off the message that I had heard from Michael McCann and there was a growing conviction within me that God wanted me to attend Harvest Bible College in Redruth, Cornwall where Dr McCann was the Principal. I did not mention these thoughts to Sylvia because I did not want to worry her unnecessarily, but as wives are prone to do, she picked up on the fact that something was playing on my mind. She quizzed me accordingly asking what it was that was bothering me.

Hesitantly I said, "I think God may be calling us to move to Cornwall".

"You must be joking!" she said incredulously.

As calmly as I could I explained to Sylvia how this had all come about, but I could understand if she was thinking, "Who is this crazy man that I am married to?"

Sylvia, seeing that I was deadly serious about this said, "If this is of God then He is going to have to show me in ways that I can understand".

Over the next few weeks God did speak to Sylvia in ways that she could understand. Firstly the Avon lady called saying it would be the last time we would be seeing her because she and her husband were selling up and moving to Cornwall to run a bed and breakfast business. Then we went to visit some friends from another church, who we only saw very rarely and they told us that they had just booked a holiday; guess where? That's right, Cornwall. Finally Ed Ryder came to see us to let us know that he and his wife Mavis had decided to sell up and move to Cornwall. Even Sylvia had to admit that all of this was probably a bit more than just a coincidence.

Now that Sylvia and I were agreed on our course of action I decided it was time to share the idea with Christian leaders and friends. To my surprise most of them did not share in my excitement, but rather could not understand why I was prepared to take what they thought was a reckless step. Undeterred, however, convinced that God was in this we decided to apply to Harvest Bible College to see if I would be granted a place. I chatted on the phone with the Secretary and arranged to go down to the College for an interview. The meeting with Michael McCann and his wife Rita went really well. They were warm and friendly and did not see the fact that I was blind as being any problem at all. They said I could take my cassette recorder into lectures and even sit my exams by whatever means was comfortable with me. I duly applied for and was accepted on to a two year Diploma course in Christian Leadership Training.

I will never forget the touching response of our friends Brian and Janet Davis when we told them what we were about to do. They said, "We don't understand why you are doing this, but we want you to know that we support you, we love you and if it turns out that it all goes wrong and even if you lose everything, our home is your home and our possessions are your possessions and we will never say 'I told you so'. That response was so liberating for us and showed us what true friendship is all about.

Of course we discussed the matter with our children, who were all excited at the prospect of going to live by the seaside. Our house in Solihull sold within a couple of days of putting it up for sale and it necessitated Sylvia going down to Cornwall with my Mum and Dad to have a look at some houses and make an offer on something which took her fancy. I trusted Sylvia implicitly to find something suitable and in the right location. She found a pleasant, modern three bedroom house in Redruth in a place called South Park. We put in an offer, which was accepted and the sale of our house in Solihull and the purchase of 60 South Park, Redruth all went through without a hitch, enabling me to have a couple of weeks to settle in before starting college.

Prior to our move, however, there was a major setback for us. My Mum had been having some difficulty for a few months in actually swallowing her food. Things would stick in her throat and she would end up having to cough until she could spit the food back out of her mouth. It was quite distressing for her. After eventually persuading her to see a doctor and attend hospital, she underwent various tests which confirmed that she was suffering from cancer of the oesophagus. There followed a course of radiotherapy, but on one hospital visit Dad and Sylvia were called in to be told by the Consultant that Mum probably only had about six months to live. It was a devastating blow for all the family, but Dad did not want Mum told that her condition was terminal and so we complied and respected his request. Of course though it did make the decision to move to Cornwall all that much more difficult to go through with. In the end I concluded that because God is sovereign this whole thing with Mum had not taken him by surprise, He knew about it all along, yet He had still called us to Cornwall. We therefore went ahead with the move, entrusting Mum and indeed the whole family into God's caring hands.

The big move 260 miles down to the South West corner of England went really well. Beverley, Sara and Allison once again settled well into their new school, though it was a little harder for Ian at Trewirge Infants. He was only there for a few months however before moving up to the junior school, where he got on much better and became a star pupil, especially excelling in sports. Ian in fact captained the school football team, scoring one amazing goal from inside his own half, when his long range shot bounced over the head of the diminutive goalkeeper. He also went on to represent West Cornwall at various age levels.

Harvest Bible College was situated in a village called Pool which separated the two, run down tin mining towns of Redruth and Camborne. To get to and from college I either had to get a lift in the car from Sylvia, or catch a bus to take me on the mile and a half journey. Just over two miles away was our nearest beach, Portreath and Sylvia loved to drive there once the children had gone off to school and I had gone to college. All in all we had some wonderful family times down at Portreath. Coming from a large industrial city like Birmingham, it was a novelty and thrill to live near so many beaches with picturesque places such as Porthtowen, Perranporth and St Ives within a half hour's drive.

My first term at Bible College went superbly and I drank in all of the lectures. The lessons were not as academic as I had imagined, but more like solid Bible teaching. At the time I was there the college had about 35 students coming from countries such as Ghana, Nigeria, India, Germany, USA and of course the United Kingdom. We became very good friends with many of the students and with a lot of them being single they used to love to come to our home and be part of a family. It was not uncommon to see Alex, Seth, Osai or Samuel stroll into our house, take off their shoes and lie down on the settee and go fast asleep.

Everyone at the college was encouraged to live by faith, trusting God for every penny. One day Alex came to me saying in a deep Afro-English tone, "Brother John I would be honoured if you would join me in prayer one night because I have a financial need". I felt deeply honoured that Alex should ask me to pray with him, because in my eyes Alex was a mighty man of prayer, as indeed were all of those students from Africa. I had a financial need too which was causing me concern as our car was in need of some urgent attention and it was no small job.

I was therefore very pleased to join Alex one night in prayer. I guessed, knowing him, that we might be praying all night and so at 10pm I said goodnight to Sylvia and informed her that I would see her in the morning. When Alex and I started to pray we were fairly quiet for a few minutes and then he got up off his knees and began to march up and down the room praying using his gift of speaking in tongues. I arose from my chair and joined him pacing the floor. We were both speaking in tongues, then singing in tongues and it was amazing to hear these two voices blending as we called out to God in worship and placing our needs before him. It was an exhilarating time as the songs and the prayers ebbed and flowed. Taking the occasional sip of water we were really going for it until about 1.15am when Alex suddenly stopped and a great peace descended on the room.

I followed his lead and sat down on a chair for a few minutes before Alex broke the silence by saying, "Thank you brother that was powerful".

"Yes it was", but why have we stopped?" I asked curiously.

"Because we got the breakthrough. Didn't you sense it?" he asked.

Well somewhat nonchalantly I said I did, but in truth I didn't. I was glad Alex was happy however and even more glad that I could unexpectedly go and join Sylvia back in our bed much earlier than anticipated.

I was shocked and thrilled then when a couple of days later I came home from college at lunchtime for Sylvia to tell me excitedly that we had received a £1,000 cheque through the post. She was a bit worried about this cheque however because instead of having a normal signature it had a little squiggle where the signature should have been, so she wondered if it was a hoax. To satisfy our curiosity I rang the Building Society concerned and they confirmed that the cheque was legitimate; it was simply that the donors wished to remain anonymous. We had been taught the practice of tithing so we decided to tithe £100 to my prayer buddy Alex and when I gave him the £100 he hugged me so tight and did a dance of delight in praise of God because he said that was the exact amount he had asked God for. Needless to say we were able to put the rest for our car repair which cost us in excess of £500.

That was just one of many thrilling examples of praying with the Africans that I experienced during our time in Cornwall. Most Friday night at the college we had an all-night prayer meeting to pray for the nations of the world and they were truly powerful times. There was also a prayer meeting Monday to Friday mornings before college at 7pm for one hour, again to pray for the nations. It was very much a college which expressed God's heart for the world.

At these prayer meetings we worked to a plan whereby we prayed for six or seven nations each day and by working to this outline we would cover all the nations of the world in a month. On one particular morning I had a remarkable experience. We were praying for what was then the Soviet Union (USSR), East and West Germany and South Africa. There were about six of us students praying and as we marched the floor of the classroom singing and praying in tongues I had a sense in my spirit of messengers from God going out to these nations and declaring "Jesus reigns". I became excited on the inside and began to sing out boldly in tongues, something I do not do lightly or often. As I sang, however, I was impressed by what sounded to me like a beautiful melody. I sensed that God was encouraging me to sing out in English and as I did some words came. I was so amazed by what came out of my mouth in poetic form that I literally ran out to get the words written down. The words that I believe came from God in such melodic form were as follows:

As the Gospel is preached / Many people they are reached

In every nation of the world Jesus reigns / Across the face of the Earth there is life and new birth

Don't you know in your heart, Jesus reigns

He is moving every hour / By the Spirit's mighty power

Sing and dance / clap your hand Jesus reigns

He is Lord of every nation / He is King of all creation

So I boldly now proclaim, Jesus reigns

He is moving in my heart / He is changing every part

I'm glad to say in me, Jesus reigns

Send me now Lord I pray / Send me now Lord today

To the world to let them know, Jesus reigns.

How awesome and thrilling it was, therefore, when a few months later we heard on the news about the break-up of Communism in the USSR, the Berlin wall coming down and Germany being reunited as one nation, followed by the end of apartheid in South Africa. The end of the 1980s was momentous and historic days in global history. It was a privilege to have had a small part to play in all of that through our prayers, along with millions of others no doubt, for the nations that God loves so very much. It seems to me that if you concern yourself with the nations then you touch God's heart in a very special way.

After we had been living in Redruth for a few months and I had got my first term at College out of the way, Mum and Dad came down to visit us. By this time all of Mum's radiotherapy treatment had finished and though she was still having a certain amount of trouble swallowing, overall she was doing quite well. To our surprise, however, Dad said that he and Mum would like to attend church with us. Harvest Bible College had some very nice modern facilities with lecture rooms and an auditorium that would seat up to 400 people. Some years earlier they had launched a church called Harvest Christian Fellowship which comprised the students plus families and individuals from the locality.

The services were always lively and inspiring with time being made at some point for the sick to be prayed for. Mum and Dad came along to one Sunday service and though the style must have been alien to them, they coped with it pretty well and Mum was prayed for by the assistant pastor, a really nice guy by the name of Mark Van Gundy. Mark was from Orlando, Florida and he was married to Mary from just up the road in Camborne. Mark very kindly asked my Mum if she would like him to come to our house to pray for her and she said that she would.

A few days later Mark duly arrived and prayed for Mum in our lounge. He was very gentle and compassionate, saying to Mum that of course one day we will all die physically and stand before God. He said how important it was that we were healed spiritually and that the Bible calls that being born again. He simply explained the good news and quoted a verse from Romans 10:13 "Whoever calls on the name of the Lord shall be saved". Mum had very little understanding of the Bible but Mark explained things as clearly as I have ever heard anyone and Mum indicated that she understood and wanted to call upon the name of Jesus to save her. Mark then led her in a prayer of commitment to Jesus Christ and from that moment on I knew that Mum, (who I had prayed for over 18 years) was now saved.

Just under 10 weeks later on 23rd August 1986 Mum passed into the presence of God to be with Jesus for ever and her suffering was over. That morning Ian and I were with Mum as we were in Birmingham for a few days. I had the privilege of praying with Mum that morning before she went to hospital where she died that evening. Mum's funeral service was conducted by Pastor Morrison, our old Irish Pastor from the Kingstanding Elim Church. It was a fine service and the Pastor gave a very inspiring Gospel address and tribute to Mum. I know that one of Mum's brothers, my Uncle Harry, was very intrigued by the message, himself having overcome bowel cancer many years earlier. He had also said that he was a bit worried about me because on the day of Mum's funeral he had seen me hugging several men rather than the more socially acceptable handshake. I explained to him that within the Church it was not unusual to greet one another, be they male or female, with a warm and friendly hug.

All this clearly left a vivid impression on my Uncle because about two years after Mum's death, I received a phone call in Cornwall from Auntie Audrey to say that Uncle Harry had been taken into hospital with a recurrence of his cancer problems and he wanted to speak with the Pastor who had conducted Mum's funeral. My sister Susan was able to make contact with Pastor Morrison, who gladly went to visit my Uncle in hospital and in so doing answer some heart-searching questions that Uncle Harry had on his mind. The glorious upshot of this was that Pastor Morrison was able to lead Uncle Harry and Auntie Audrey to Jesus. I took great comfort from the fact that Mum had not only received the gift of eternal life weeks before she died, but in her passing, it also led directly to her brother and his wife coming to the Lord also.

Whilst I was still enjoying myself at College, the church side of things was going well too. By way of a change of strategy, it was decided by the leadership of the church to introduce three house groups meeting midweek so that people could come together for prayer, mutual encouragement and pastoral support. Sylvia and I were asked to lead a group in our home, which we agreed to do. Most weeks we had about 15 people gathering, including three of the African contingent to add a bit of fervour and also I am pleased to say, Daniel and Deborah, former students at the College who were now part of the Bible College staff. They were good teachers in their own right and Daniel was also a very fine worship leader. We had been in Cornwall for about six months when we became aware that across the road from the Bible College a new estate was being built. It looked very nice indeed and out of interest, nothing more, we decided to go and have a look around the show house. As we entered it, I felt instinctively this was the kind of house of which I dreamed. Not that it was a mansion you understand. When I was back in Solihull and praying about moving to Cornwall I had a definite idea of the kind of house, layout and style that I would like.

Due to the fact that our house in Solihull sold so rapidly, however, we had to move quickly in order not to lose the sale. This meant of course that we had to buy somewhere pretty hastily and in that regard Sylvia (with Mum and Dad's help) did a great job in finding South Park. We were happy at South Park overall, other than it was a little on the small side, had night storage heaters which we really did not like and there was that awkward little journey to and from college each day. Nothing major, but I did feel a stirring of faith for these new houses across the road from the college on a small estate called Treloweth Gardens. There was a plot available for this soon to be erected four bedroom house. We took away the details to mull over, but we felt it was about £10,000 above what we could realistically afford.

The following night at house group we were drawing to a close and Sylvia went into the kitchen to make drinks. We were finishing off with a short time of music as Daniel gently played his guitar. Once again I had that experience of singing out in tongues and then finding the Holy Spirit prompting me to give the interpretation in English. I did it again as a song and the words were as follows:

I want to do something crazy / I want to do something good.

I want to do something crazy for you Lord

To love you, to trust you / To depend upon your Word.

I want to do something crazy for you Lord."

With that Deborah rushed out into the kitchen to tell Sylvia what I had just sung. She confided that she and Daniel were thinking about doing something crazy. They felt God was calling them to step out in faith to buy a bungalow even though they had no money. Deborah pulled out of her bag some sales particulars of a bungalow they were interested in and would you believe it? It was on Treloweth Gardens, where we had been looking. Sylvia then pulled out our details and showed Deborah resulting in Deborah and Sylvia embracing in fits of laughter at what seemed to be two crazy ideas.

Daniel and Deborah were greatly loved at church and college and once news got around that they were looking to buy a property, we took up what we call a love offering one Sunday in church and raised enough money to enable them to have a deposit. As a qualified pharmacist, Daniel was successful in getting a part time job at a pharmacy in Camborne and as a result they were able to obtain a mortgage and move into their bungalow.

In our case, were we ready to move again only a year after moving from Solihull and also could we afford to do so. There was the thought of what will people back in the West Midlands think if we move again, though when we prayed about the matter, it was as though God was saying, "If you've got the faith, I've got the house". No one that we spoke to said that the house was overly extravagant for a family of our size and it would have several advantages to it. One thing about being at the College was that we were surrounded by people of faith and the Word of God and that made it so much easier to take steps that ordinarily might seem beyond us. So we decided to stretch our faith our little further and move from South Park to 25 Townfield, Pool, just two minutes' walk from college and church.

The first answer to prayer was that we were granted a mortgage with me being a student and only having a limited amount of support from people around the country. Fortunately the Building society Manager was a Christian and he was fully conversant with the term 'living by faith'. We decided that we would take in a student to help us with the increased mortgage that we were embarking on. Once all the paperwork had gone through and we knew we were actually buying the property, it was fun visiting the plot to see the house being built brick by brick. The other astonishing thing about this was that we did not know until all the paperwork had been processed that Michael and Rita McCann, Principals of the Bible College had actually bought the property next door. How would they feel having one of their students living next door we wondered?

As it turned out Mike and Rita were absolutely fine about this and on the day of our move we even had some of the students give us a helping hand. I have to say that of all the houses we have lived in this was my personal favourite. For me it was my dream house. It was detached so I could play my records as loud as I liked without fear of upsetting the neighbours and we had a lovely big garden that we could stroll around, playing football, cricket and tennis whenever we liked. We also had a double garage which left us plenty of room for storage, plus of course leaving room for my car, should I miraculously get my eyesight back!

Healings, heartbreak and homecoming

During our time in Cornwall we experienced some truly miraculous healings, one of which happened to Sylvia in our new house. Sylvia had been troubled with lower back pain for a couple of years, there were days when it was very bad indeed. Most days she had to roll out of bed in the morning and crawl around the floor until her back loosened up.

One night a party of students were going over to a small church in Penryn, near Falmouth to watch a video of the American healing evangelist Benny Hinn. Sylvia agreed to take her car with me and three other students on board. We watched the video and in truth it was pretty amazing stuff and at the end of that service many people on the video testified to being healed by the power of God. The Pastor, Patrick Stevenson, who also taught at Harvest Bible College, said that the same power that we saw displayed on the video was present that night to heal people in that little church in Cornwall. He invited anyone who needed to receive healing to go forward for prayer. I could have gone forward of course but didn't. Rather I was hoping that Sylvia would go forward for prayer because her condition was giving her far much more stress than my lack of sight was giving me. Sylvia, however, stayed rooted to the spot and afterwards she told me that even though what we saw on the video was pretty incredible, she remained dubious as to whether that same power could be transmitted to that little church in Penryn.

Next morning I was downstairs when Sylvia called me from the bedroom to say that she had no back pain and it wasn't even stiff. Doubters, that we were, thought to ourselves, perhaps this was just one of those rare good mornings. The fact is that nearly 20 years later, Sylvia's back is stronger than ever. She has worked for the past 12 years in nursing homes and a hospice and much of that work is really heavy. She could not have done this kind of work had not God graciously and miraculously healed her back. I can only conclude that he did it out of his great grace and because he loves her so much, not because she had faith because, as she would tell you, she most certainly did not.

My first year at Bible College went brilliantly. I loved everything about it. The lectures were good and I did well in my exams. The church, Harvest Christian Fellowship was good too and we had the benefit of hearing some really fine speakers including Jason Peebles from Atlanta, Georgia and a guy called Robert Massbach, originally from Holland but now working in the UK. Our four children had all settled well into school and they were also enjoying church life, especially with there being so many young students. It was a happy time and we enjoyed taking our many visitors from back home in Birmingham to some of the lovely seaside resorts around West Cornwall.

I mentioned earlier that in order to help us with the increased mortgage payments we would have to take in a lodger. Our first student was Raid Thaglag, a Jordanian young man who was studying aeronautic engineering at the Cornwall College in Pool. Raid, a Muslim, was with us for close on a year and he was on the whole an ideal first lodger for us. Meal times were always lively occasions with endless chatter, debates and occasionally arguments. One night Raid said that he would give anything to have a meal in silence, but he doubted that our girls could stay quiet for more than a few minutes. After some discussion about this, Raid said, "I'll give you £5 each if you can stay quiet for 10 minutes".

Well, no more incentive was needed and the deal was struck. We enjoyed the quietest meal we have ever had in our household that night and Raid true to his word paid out £5 to each of our kids later that evening. Raid was a good sport and he mixed well with the students from the Bible College. More than once he said that he felt as though he was part of a big family. When it came to say farewell to Raid at the end of his academic year we threw a party for him and invited a couple of his Muslim friends from college and also a dozen or so of the Bible students. At the end of what was a lovely evening we were able to pray for Raid and send him on his way with the Lord's blessing.

Our second student was a young lady, Carolyn Dowding from Guernsey, and she was in Cornwall to taking a qualification in nursery nursing. In fact it turned out that she was on the same course as our own daughter Allison. Just like Raid, Carolyn turned out to be brilliant and in fact she became in her own way quite a good friend to Sylvia, almost a fourth daughter. She fitted in so well with our family and it was a real pleasure to have her around.

It's hard to identify at which point things started to go wrong, but go wrong they did and big style. I was well into my second year as a bible student when my ear problem, which had settled down for a few years, suddenly flared up again. A trip to the Doctors led to me being referred to hospital in Truro and then to another Consultant in Plymouth. I was having so much time off at that stage for investigations that it was agreed to give me the term off in order to concentrate on getting my ear sorted and then do that term again the following year. To this day I cannot explain why this offensive smell occurred in my ear, I underwent tests for cancer, which thankfully turned out to be negative and there was even talk of operating but the dangers of facial paralysis were too great so it was decided to leave things alone. The anatomical structure inside the left ear gave cause for concern, as I had found out almost 10 years earlier when they had discovered that jugular bulb, and eventually it was decided that I should attend Trelisk Hospital in Truro every Saturday morning to have the ear cleaned. I am happy to say that a few years down the line, when back in Birmingham, I underwent a mastoid operation which rectified the problem of the offensive odour and in so doing also managed to improve my hearing on the left side too. Instead of once a week I now only have to attend hospital for an ear check once a year so that is a spectacular improvement.

During those months of uncertainty, particularly once the word cancer had been mentioned, one of those fears that I wrote about at the beginning of this book, started to invade my mind once again. One night I had a most vivid dream about my own funeral and I awoke at about 6am sweating and shaking with fear. I was relieved to find that I was still alive. I immediately got up and went downstairs to pray. I dropped to my knees and buried my head into the armchair as I cried out to God. "Please God, help me" I cried, "deal with this fear and sort out the ear problem for me".

As I bowed there in desperation, I experienced another of those all too rare moments when it is as though God speaks right into your heart. This is what I felt God was saying, "You can lie down and die or you can stand up and live – the choice is yours".

It was sharp and like an arrow to my heart. I responded at once by standing like a soldier to attention and I said back to God, "I choose to stand up and live". A Scripture came to my mind straightaway from Psalm 118 "I shall not die, but I shall live to declare your works oh Lord."

Ever since then that has been my watchword. I have breath this day but only in order that I may declare the works of God. That is my primary purpose for being alive here on Planet Earth. During that term I was off, however, things began to happen at the Bible College of an alarming nature. Some members of staff walked out, whilst others were dismissed amid rumours of homosexuality and financial irregularities etc. We had already picked up on certain things that were being said by other Church leaders and Christians locally, but those things only confirmed misgivings that Sylvia had been having for months. There was also a suspicion that one of the students was a paedophile, which was a big shock because he had actually become quite a good friend to us and our kids. He was however convicted a few years later and sent to prison. The sad fact began to dawn on me that I would not be able to go back to Bible College. I remember walking the streets around Treloweth Gardens and with a heavy heart crying out to God "Oh why has this happened, all I wanted to do was to study your Word?"

By this time Sylvia and I had become really good friends with two young couples who had come to Bible College, John and Wendy Oldham and Phil and Christine Jenkins from Rochdale and Oldham respectively. They had been good friends for many years. At that point they had no children and we just hit it off together and our kids liked them too which was a big plus. They had also become concerned about a number of aspects within the college and the church. After some discussion, I decided to contact Steve Wood, who you may recall I mentioned earlier when I first heard him speak in Leicester. He was the leading Elder at Solihull Christian Fellowship and one of those four who had broken away over the issue of direction. Steve had since moved to the South West and was living in Wells, and is now an Elder at Bath City Church.

It was agreed that John, Phil and I would travel up to Wells to chat and pray with Steve. We talked over our concerns with him and spent a good deal of time praying together. Steve set out some things for us to think about and consider carefully. He did add that if we were to leave then we should request a meeting with Dr McCann to explain why it was that we could no longer be part of the Bible College or the church. Steve said that we owed Michael that as a brother in Christ, to be honest and to walk in the light with him. There was no doubt in our mind that we had to leave and so an appointment was made. I attended with Sylvia and though I was nervous I knew that I did not want to cause trouble but simply to share my heart. Despite our decision, I did have a love in my heart for Michael and Rita and no one was more upset than me at the way things were working out.

As we entered the Principal's office, Michael was sat behind a huge desk with his Dean of Students at his side.

"Come in John and Sylvia, sit yourselves down" Michael said in his usual upbeat way.

We took our seats, and I then went on to explain the reasons why I could not continue to be a student at the Bible College and why it was that we as a family would be leaving the church. I did stress to Michael that I had really appreciated all of the good things that we as a family had received in the time that we had been there and that we did love him and Rita. Michael said how sorry he was to be losing us and how unfortunate it was that we had listened to gossip. After a brief handshake we left Michael's office and over the course of the next few months one by one people continued to leave the College and the church.

It was around this time that a series of terrible events started happening, and had it not been for the support of our friends John and Wendy, Phil and Christine and Daniel and Deborah, who had all joined the exodus away from Harvest, I dare not think what may have happened to us. It all began one morning just after 9am when there was a ring on the front doorbell. I opened the door to hear this lady say, "Hello John, it's Florence Bailey, I'm here with a police officer because your Ian has been involved in an accident".

It was one of those moments when time seems to stand still and you don't feel as if what you are hearing is really happening. Anyway Sylvia was at the top of the stairs, inquisitively wondering who was calling at that time of the morning, but once she heard the words police officer and accident she was down in a flash. Florence and the policeman came inside and the officer said, "Your son was involved in an accident with a bus while crossing the road to school. He has suffered a head injury but we do not know how serious it is. He has been taken to hospital in Truro so if you would like to get your things together we will take you".

By this time Sylvia was in tears and being cuddled by Florence, whose son David, was a friend of Ian's. All I knew to do was to ask if we could pray before we set off for the hospital. Sylvia, Florence, the policeman and I stood there all holding hands in a circle and I prayed for Ian, the bus driver and for the staff at the hospital that all would be well. It transpired that Ian had been listening to a tape of the U2 album *Rattle and Hum* on his personal stereo and he had stepped out to cross the road to school, but he had done so in front of a park vehicle. Unfortunately there was a coach coming passed the stationary vehicle and it glanced the side of Ian's head, ripping his right ear almost totally off. Subsequently all personal stereos, or walkmans, as they were more commonly called in those days, were banned in the school. By the time we arrived at the hospital in Truro, Ian was already in the operating theatre as no time could be wasted when it came to sewing the ear back on. Thankfully the operation was a complete success and incredibly Ian was out in three days recuperating at home, enjoying his many cards, presents and visitors from school. One of the doctors at the hospital said to Ian, "Do you know young man, you are the first person I have met who has collided with a bus and lived to tell the tale".

Shortly after that Allison was returning home from a night out with Matthew, her surfer boyfriend and they had a nasty experience on one of the coastal roads when his van veered off the road and into a ditch. In the same time span Sylvia, who had been driving for 15 years then without the hint of an accident had two in successive nights. On both occasions she was fetching lads, including Ian, from school football games, one in Truro and one in Camborne. On each occasion Sylvia was waiting at traffic lights when someone bumped into the back of her. Again we say it thankfully, no one was hurt, but Sylvia was shaken emotionally and by now we were all beginning to wonder what was happening to us. Not long after that we had a new car, but not for long as I will reveal.

From time to time I would receive invitations to go and preach in churches back in Birmingham and other parts too including Rochdale and Oldham thanks to my friends John and Phil. On one of those occasions I was preaching at Castle Bromwich Community Church in Birmingham. Sylvia and the children meanwhile stayed with friends in Solihull and attended Solihull Christian Fellowship to try and meet up with as many acquaintances as possible. After I had finished preaching, I closed the service with a prayer, but before I could sit down, the Pastor came and stood alongside me and said that he wanted to pray for me. Before he did so he placed a set of keys into one of my hands. I said, "What are those for?"

He replied by saying that these were the keys for our new car. Yes you're right it was another one of those déjà vu moments. This was a very well planned manoeuvre. The whole of Castle Bromwich Community Church was in on this big surprise and I was led outside of the Community Centre, where the service had been held. When out in the fresh air I was taken to a beautiful blue Volkswagen Passat. I was told that this was now our family car and when I asked incredulously how this had come about, I was told to speak with Dr Gordon Coleman for the full story. I was driven by Dave the Pastor of the church over to Solihull, with his wife Glenys following at the rear.

When we arrived in Solihull there were a whole load of people including Gordon and Julia, plus Sylvia and our four children waiting to greet us. Sylvia at this stage had no idea what was going on and it was left to me to have the joy of breaking this exciting news to her. So it was that we had travelled up in an old Vauxhall Viva but we were travelling back in a much more modern Volkswagen Passat. What had happened was that Gordon had become aware of our need of a more reliable car and so he had contacted some of the local churches where I regularly preached, made the need known to them and asked if they would make a donation towards purchasing a newer vehicle. So the God of surprises had turned up again and just when we needed some encouragement after all the difficulties we had encountered in the previous few months. The joy was short-lived however.

By now our three girls had left school and whilst Allison was at college, Beverley and Sara went into the retail trade. As teenagers do of course they also got into the night life and very often this meant Sylvia dropping them off, or more often than not picking them up from somewhere late at night. One particular night Beverley went out into Camborne with her boyfriend Ian and because he could drive and we were, as we mistakenly thought, insured for any driver, we gave him the car keys to drive Beverley home, thus avoiding the necessity for Sylvia to go out late at night. Sylvia had just gone up to bed at about 11pm when the front door opened and Beverley came rushing in, crying hysterically saying "Dad, Dad I'm so sorry, I've crashed the car." She could hardly get her words out for sobbing.

Sylvia came running down the stairs to find out what had happened. Apparently on the way home Ian had asked Beverley if she wanted an impromptu driving lesson. With her agreement Ian drove into the car park of Cornwall College before allowing Beverley to take the steering wheel. How it happened I don't exactly know, but I think Beverley put her foot on the accelerator instead of the brake pedal, causing the car to mount a verge, go over the garden area and into

162

a brick wall. Beverley then ran home to tell us what had happened, leaving Ian to try and clear up some of the mess. Sylvia went back to the scene of the accident with Beverley and together with Ian managed to get the car off the garden and back around the corner to our garage. It was only later after I had broken the news to Gordon that I found out the car was only insured third party, whereas previously we had always insured our cars fully comprehensive any driver. So it was that our lovely new car had been written off within a couple of weeks, but the overriding and important factor was that nobody had been hurt. The car was gone, but we still had Beverley fully intact. A painful and expensive lesson had been learned not for the first time, or the last by the Flanner family.

After leaving Harvest we had a total rest from Church for a month or two though eventually we did visit a couple of local churches. At that point, however, I had to conclude that we were beaten, battered and bruised by events and were mostly happy to stay at home. Together with our friends John and Wendy, Phil and Christine, and Daniel and Deborah however, we did meet together for prayer and arising out of that we decided that we would like to organise a Gospel concert in the area featuring an artist we all admired, Bryn Haworth. Bryn is a magnificent exponent of the slide guitar, who has featured on many hit albums and singles, most notably *Baker Street* by Jerry Rafferty. We wrote to Bryn to check out his fee and whether he would be willing to come to our area. He was keen to break new ground in West Cornwall and so we agreed to go ahead and arrange the concert. We booked the main hall at Cornwall College and after a slow start the tickets sales really picked up so that on the night we had over 200 people in for what was a memorable evening.

Bryn and his wife Sally stayed with us in our home, but sadly the mantle of being a great guitar player did not rub off on me in any way, shape or form. In publicising the concert for Bryn however, it gave me the chance to make contact with BBC Radio Cornwall and even take part in an interview. Later I also had the chance to co-present a Country Gospel programme on the station with their regular Country music presenter in those days Chris Phipps. It was great to get involved with radio once again.

By this time our next door neighbours Michael and Rita McCann had gone off to America on an extended preaching tour, but in their absence we were all surprised to find that Harvest Bible College was closed down, along with

Harvest Christian Fellowship. With the fallout from Harvest there were a lot of Christians going nowhere as far as church was concerned. A few of us did start meeting in our home to start with and then in Redruth Community Centre on a Sunday afternoon. We were attracting between 25 and 30 people. We were blessed in having some excellent musicians amongst us. Daniel played guitar, as did Wendy and Christine, who could also sing. John was a gifted drummer and then we were joined by Ian and Jackie Langridge, together with their three young boys. We also had several gifted speakers in our midst as well including Phil and Deborah so all in all we had a pretty strong nucleus of solid Christian people. For practical reasons we gave ourselves the name of Redruth Community Church and I do believe that things could have taken off and God could have raised up a pretty significant local church in that area. Perhaps it had all come just a little bit too soon after the major disappointment of what had happened at Harvest.

The events outlined above were certainly taking their toll on our marriage. Rows became the order of the day, often with the kids involved too and our once happy home began to more resemble a war zone than a loving Christian family. Then came the hammer blow as Sylvia announced that she was leaving as she could not take any more. At that point she did not know if she was leaving for good or just for a break. All I know is that she was going to live with her Mum and Dad back in Birmingham for a while. The day Sylvia left I remember being overwhelmed with a sense of grief and failure. After the first couple of days, which felt really strange, I actually started to enjoy myself. It was quite nice actually to be able to do what I wanted to do without having to think about anyone else first. I know that sounds selfish, but that's just how it was. I had time for me. I did have the kids of course, but Beverley, Sara and Allison were pretty independent by now and Ian was very little trouble. I think, on reflection, it was a very precious time for all of us and I don't know how long we would have stayed in that state had not God intervened once again.

Right out of the blue we received a cheque for £200 through the post from New Life Church in Solihull, suggesting that we use it to book a place with them at the Wales Bible Week to be held a few weeks later in Builth Wells. I spoke with Sylvia on the phone to explain what had happened and within a few days she returned to be with us back in Cornwall. Only a few days after Sylvia had returned to us we spent a lovely day on the beach at Portreath, soaking up the sunshine, with the Stevenson family. It was while chatting there that Pat said to us that some of the events of the previous two years had affected him to the point where he had almost felt like giving up. He said ruefully, "I think I need to be literally picked up and dropped in the middle of a large worship meeting. Maybe then the flame will be rekindled."

I heard the cry of Pat's heart and is saddened me to see this man of God, normally so full of joy, as crestfallen as he was. Later that day I was on the phone to Steve Wood talking about another issue altogether and as our conversation drew to a close, Steve said, "Oh by the way, how are Pat and Josie doing?"

"Funny you should ask" I said and then went on to relate what had happened to them and our conversation on the beach earlier in the day.

A few days later I had a very excited Pat Stevenson on the phone saying that they had received a generous cheque from Steve Wood's church in Somerset with the suggestion that they attend the Wales Bible Week with the Flanner's. It all happened very quickly and before we knew it there we were as two families sharing a tent in Builth Wells. I know that Sylvia found that one of the hardest weeks of her life, attending all of these joyful meetings and meeting all these people when on the inside she was feeling so screwed up emotionally. For all that, however, we did have plenty of laughs especially in the tent at night. The Stevenson's were clearly amazed by the week and the warmth of the friendship they experienced from folk on the site. As we lay on our beds, divided of course by curtains, we chatted long into the night trying to fathom where things had gone wrong at Harvest.

On returning home from the Bible Week family life was much more peaceful though there was a growing sense that our time in Cornwall would soon be over. Sylvia and I decided to go up to Wells to spend a few days at Beckington Cottage with Steve and Jeanne Wood. The Wood's home at the top of a hill, overlooked the quaint historic city of Wells with its cobblestone streets and majestic Cathedral. We spent a very pleasant couple of days there, talking over our situation and tapping into their wisdom. At the end of it, we were all of one mind that we needed to move back to Solihull in order for me to find employment, to be back among family and friends and most important of all for the good of our marriage.

Our decision to leave Cornwall led to an exodus of our friends too. John and Wendy and Phil and Christine went back up North to their former churches, whilst Daniel and Deborah moved back to Michigan in the United States, where Daniel began working for a pharmacy within a large hospital. Currently they live in Virginia and they have three children, Grace, Abigail and Jonathan. We are still often in touch, especially by email. John is now Pastor of Emmanuel Christian Fellowship in Rochdale whilst Wendy is working as an audiologist. They have three kids, Joshua, James and Hannah. I have the privilege of going to preach there on around four occasions each year. Phil and Christine after a few years back home decided to up and move once again and are currently living in Bradford on Avon. They have three children too, Charis, Simon and Kay and they attend Bath City Church, where Steve Wood is now one of the Elders. Ian and Jackie, with their three boys who have now grown up, stayed in Cornwall and attend Truro Vineyard Church.

Our own family had mixed feelings about us deciding to leave Cornwall. Beverley had just moved away from home to Dursely in Gloucestershire with her then boyfriend Ian. He was working for a Building Society whilst Beverley got a job as a sales assistant with River Island. Allison was settled into her nursery nursing course and decided to stay to complete that and we did find leaving her behind extraordinarily hard. Sara, who then worked for Texas Homecare, decided that she would give that up and go back to Solihull with us and Ian was just excited at the prospect of being closer to Aston Villa once again – clearly destined to be a man after my own heart!

I found it very difficult putting our house at Townfield, Treloweth Gardens up for sale. As I said earlier, it was my dream house and I loved it there. It had to be done however as it was well over a year since I had left the Bible College and I had not even been able to get myself a sniff of a job interview. With all the moving costs considered we made quite substantial financial losses, which left us thinking that maybe the people who said we should not move to Cornwall in the first place were right after all. Even with the benefit of hindsight, however, I still cannot say whether it was the right or wrong thing to do. What I do know is that our motives were pure in wanting to serve God and in doing that we have learned some very valuable lessons, albeit at a price.

Returns and revivals

After unsuccessfully trying to buy property in other parts of Solihull, we eventually gravitated back to Damsonwood and bought a house only about 200 yards from the one we had sold. Draycote Close is a quiet little cul-de-sac, where at least I know my way around and am familiar with the bus routes, shops etc. There was a two month gap between selling our house in Cornwall and being able to move into Draycote Close, so rather than risk losing the sale, some friends of ours very kindly agreed to put Sylvia, Ian and me up for a while. We spent eight weeks or so in the home of Richard and Audrey Akers and their two boys Stuart and Graham. Very pleasant it was too. We ate out a lot in those times, particularly at a pub called The Orange Tree located in a village called Chadwick End. Sara joined us too for those treats as she was living with my sister Joan, who also lived in Solihull.

When we eventually got to move into Draycote Close, thankfully there was hardly any work which needed to be done so that was nice and it helped us settle in all the more quickly. After quite a bit of soul-searching we decided that we would go back to Solihull Christian Fellowship rather than New Life Church. This was hard on Richard and Audrey because they were at New Life Church and could reasonably have expected us to go there in light of the love which they had shown us. What clinched it in the end though was probably a visit from one of the Solihull Christian Fellowship Elders, Dave Wort. Dave made it clear that it was lovely to have us back in the area and if we were still looking for a church then we would be most welcome back at Solihull Christian Fellowship, where we had a lot of friends and there would be no pressure. We would just be free to relax and enjoy the love of God. It sounded good and in truth it was for quite a few years.

When it came to me finding a job this was proving difficult. Since I last worked in an office things had moved on as far as technology was concerned. No longer the manual typewriter, or indeed the electric typewriter. No, in the short time I had been away many offices had now gone over to personal computers or PCs as they were more commonly known. After discussions with my Disability Officer at the local Job Centre, it was decided that I should apply to go on a Business Administration course at Queen Alexandra College in Harborne, Birmingham. This was a specialist college of further education offering a wide range of courses for people not just with visual impairment but also a number of other disabilities too. Within a couple of weeks of my application I heard that I had been accepted on to the course and started soon afterwards. The course involved me learning a number of skills including telephony, reception work, brushing up on my audio typing skills and what was to become very important to me, word processing with the aid of speech based screen-reading software. I wasn't using Job Access With Speech (JAWS) software then, but a system called Hal which was (and still is) produced by a company called Dolphin. This was also pre-Microsoft Windows and I was using WordStar in DOS format. It was amazing to me to be using screen-reading software and even though it was a synthesised voice, its monotonous robotic tone did not bother me at all. I loved the extra freedom to be able to listen to and correct my own documents the synthesiser gave me.

I thoroughly enjoyed my year at Queen Alexandra College, achieving good grades in all of the modules that I studied, but I especially did well at and loved word processing. Queen Alexandra College has a great reputation for high standards of education and I have to say the food in the dining room wasn't bad either! Towards the end of my year I attended two weeks work placement at the Birmingham Housing Department and that was fun. Following the placement, our head of department, Theresa Napier, said that the college had received an invitation from a local Rotary Club to attend one of their fund-raising dinners. At the dinner they wanted to hear from two or three of the students about what course they had undertaken and what kind of employment they were looking for. Theresa wondered if I would be willing to give the final talk of the evening summing things up for about 15 minutes. Of course I agreed saying I would consider it an honour.

I had never been to a Rotary-type dinner before and so it was quite an experience, with a number of distinguished people being applauded to their tables – we weren't among them I hasten to add! I was very pleased with the way my talk went too. I was able to pay an apt tribute to the work being done by all of the staff at Queen Alexandra College as well as place myself in the proverbial shop window for any would-be employers. It worked a treat too because after the dinner as we mingled with other guests, I was approached by one of the businessmen present.

"That was a pretty fine speech" said the man as he shook my hand warmly. "I have a vacancy for an audio typist if you are interested. I run an Estate Agents business in Kings Heath."

Needless to say I was all ears as the man went on, "My name is Peter Cariss and I would like to arrange for you to visit my premises so that we can talk if you are interested in the job that is?"

In the absence of any other offers of work it transpired that I left college one Friday in the July and walked straight into the job as an audio typist/word processing operator with Cariss Residential on the following Monday. My job was basically typing up the sales particulars on a variety of properties and all in all it was very interesting work. Peter was a good employer and on occasions he would actually take his staff, including me, out to auctions. It was something that Peter certainly did not have to do, but I enjoyed it and it helped us all to feel part of the business as a whole. Sadly for us all the business ran into financial difficulties and after six months working at Cariss Residential I, along with other full time staff, were told that we would have to reduce our hours to become part time. I could not agree to that with a mortgage and other financial commitments and so I allowed Peter to make me redundant. I was only out of work for a few days however, because on the off chance I decided to pop into the Inland Revenue office in Solihull, where I had worked previously in Special Office. It must have been God's perfect timing because I discovered that there were two vacancies for audio typists and so I filled an application form out there and then (with someone's kind assistance) and submitted it immediately. A couple of days later I received a phone call inviting me for interview and thankfully I got offered a job. Praise God, the Inland Revenue had come up trumps for me once again. This time around I was destined for a longer period of service than on the two previous occasions.

Again I found the work interesting and I worked in an office with about six other people (ladies of course) and a typing manager, which was a new experience for me. Of the people I worked with Samantha, used to be at school with my daughter Beverley. She was also an avid Liverpool supporter and her knowledge of football certainly rivalled that of any man I knew. Sam, as we called her, married a tax inspector and though football was not his number one passion, Sam soon got him travelling with her up and down the M6 to Anfield as a Liverpool season ticket-holder. Another of the girls I worked with,

169

Lynnette, was very much into tap dancing and one year she was persuaded to undertake a spot of tap dancing on one of the desks in order to raise money for *Children in Need*. Perhaps the most interesting typing manager I worked for in those days (and there were quite a few) was Pat O'Kelly. I wasn't with Pat for long as she took a redundancy package with the demand for typists starting to diminish, but she was a truly wonderful personality who was very light in spirit. Pat was also the sister of Richard O'Kelly, the former Walsall footballer and West Bromwich Albion coach.

Geographically this was a great place to work because on good weather days I could walk to and from work, a distance of just about two miles, which was my attempt to reduce my expanding waistline. In actual fact that was a lovely, peaceful walk around the back of Solihull hospital and along the path at the side of Solihull School. On that journey I had many talks with God about all kinds of people and situations. On one such walk home I was caught totally unawares. When I left the office at about 4.30pm it felt like a warm, balmy evening and so I began my trek home at a fairly gentle pace. I had been walking for about 10 minutes when I felt a few spots of rain, followed by a distant clap of thunder. For a moment I thought about going back and getting the bus home, but in the end decided to press on at a much quicker pace than I had set off. It now began to look distinctly dark, even to my eyes. The rain became heavier and heavier and the thunder drew ever closer. It seemed as if I was the only person out walking that afternoon because I did not pass another soul on that journey. However as the rain lashed down I became drenched through to the skin and I could hardly walk because of the rain running into and irritating my eyes. I began to feel quite distressed in the sense that I had lost my way. I could not locate the alleyway that I was supposed to go down. The rain was so loud and my senses were so dulled with the cold and the wet that I became hopelessly disorientated.

To my great relief, after about a 20 minute downpour, the rain subsided as quickly as it had come and I was able to find my way home. I just remember getting home, cold and wet to hear Sylvia say sympathetically "My love, you're soaked!"

"Indeed I am" I said, "thoroughly soaked".

It turned out to be quite a profound moment for me because God spoke to me and said that this was kind of a parable. God showed me that He wants His people, that is, those who love Him, to be soaked in His Holy Spirit. He said to me that He pours out His Holy Spirit like rain and He wants us to be drenched even to the point where we become disorientated just as I did. He said that we rely too much on our own abilities and not enough on His abilities. People are far too content with a touch of God in their lives instead of allowing Him to consume or soak them. Anyway I am sure you get the analogy and for me that was quite a defining moment.

During this period things were going along quite nicely at Solihull Christian Fellowship. I was leading one of the house groups on Damsonwood where we were living along with seven or eight other families. At that juncture there were two Elders serving in the church, Alan Cameron and David Wort, two long-standing friends of ours. It was a big surprise to me when I was invited to prayerfully consider becoming part of the Eldership of the church. I say it was a surprise because I did not consider myself the type of character to become an Elder. My experience had been that Elders were serious-minded, cautious type of people whose children were all good and regularly attending church. I certainly did not fit that image. I love to be spontaneous, can occasionally be flippant, and have a 'carry on' type sense of humour and following the debacle in Cornwall, my children rarely went to church.

I talked about my misgivings, especially with Alan and in so doing asked what it was they felt I would bring to the Eldership. I was told that I would bring qualities such as faith, inspiration and love to the church, along with a wealth of experience. After careful consideration and talking through with Sylvia I eventually agreed and was duly brought into Eldership along with another friend of many years, Pall Singh. Pall, as his name would suggest, is from a Sikh background and was converted in his late teens in the Handsworth area of Birmingham. Pall and his wife Joy are now actively involved in supporting people from an Asian background who are seeking to live out their lives as Christians. Shortly after becoming an Elder of Solihull Christian Fellowship it became apparent that something phenomenal was happening in the wider Christian Church. It got labelled and will certainly go down in history as the Toronto Blessing.

Toronto Airport Vineyard Church were together for a prayer meeting in 1994, I believe it was Father's Day there. On that night God turned up in an amazing way and began to touch lives. Obviously it was one of those times that is hard to describe even if you had been there, but there are plenty of reports of what happened at that time. Suffice to say that lives were changed for good. God's presence became so real in that meeting that nobody wanted to leave. The Pastors of what is now called Toronto Airport Church, John and Carol Arnott, decided that if God wanted to meet with His people then they should continue to gather together night after night and that is what has happened ever since.

Initially it was just folk from that church who met, then folk from nearby churches started to join in, but as news of what God was doing each night spread further, people started to travel from all over Canada and North America. Gradually the phenomena spread across the globe and as people travelled to the Toronto Airport Church to be in the presence of God they testified to being greatly refreshed, have a deeper understanding of the Father heart of God and be emotionally and physically healed. To date hundreds of thousands of people have travelled from across the world and met God afresh, or even for the first time, in that seemingly insignificant church at Toronto Airport.

One night a Christian friend by the name of Elizabeth said that she had heard a taped message which had had a profound effect upon her. Clearly enthused by what she had heard, Elizabeth dropped the tape into our porch one afternoon for us to listen to. It was a tape of a recorded message given by a lady by the name of Ellie Mumford, wife of a Pastor from London by the name of John Mumford. On this tape Ellie (who sounds a bit like Queen Elizabeth II) was describing her visit to Toronto and the impact it had had on her.

I have to say that Sylvia is not really one for listening to tapes, but on this occasion she said, "Let's have an early night and listen to Ellie Mumford in bed".

The offer was too good for me to resist. We listened with baited breath, hanging on to Ellie's every word. On occasions we found ourselves laughing heartily and at other times the tears were streaming down our face as the love of God touched our hearts. It was really beautiful and the only reason we did not sleep well that night was because in our hearts we were so exhilarated. We decided before going to sleep that we would play this tape at our house group meeting in our home a couple of nights later, but we had no idea the incredible impact it was going to have.

There were 10 of us gather in our lounge that night and after one or two worship songs and a quick burst of prayer it was time for me to introduce the tape. It is not always easy for people sitting around in someone's lounge to listen to a cassette tape, much easier if it is video or nowadays DVD. Anyway I did stress that this was something very special and it did only last for half an hour or so. As soon as Ellie began to speak you could tell that folk were right with it. Just as with Sylvia and me a couple of nights earlier, there was laughter and tears.

At the end of the message Ellie asked people to stand for prayer. Immediately everyone in our lounge stood up and that was unusual in itself. Then Ellie began to pray and I heard a thud as one of the ladies in the group fell to the floor. I obviously looked concerned, but Sylvia reassured me that everything was okay. Then Colin, one of our dear friends began to laugh infectiously (so unlike Colin to draw attention to himself in that way). One by one around the room different ones began to be touched by the Holy Spirit, including Eileen, a lady in her 70's from a very strict wing of the Christian Church, who began to shake from head to toe. It really was an astonishing evening when God turned up in a way that I had never known before or since. We usually wound things up at around 10.30 but nobody wanted to leave and it was midnight before we were able to persuade the last person to go.

All Ellie Mumford does on this tape is to talk about her visit to the Toronto Church and the impact that it had upon her. It seems as if everywhere that tape is played similar things happen in that God turns up and blesses people. That indeed is a characteristic of this 'Toronto Blessing' in that if you have received something then you have an ability to give it away to others and the more you give it away the more you get back. One man in our church by the name of John had suffered on and off from depression for many years. He asked Dave Wort, Sylvia and I to go and pray with him. We went to his home and the moment we reached out to pray for him he fell on the floor and began to roll around laughing like a baby. He laughed and laughed with his legs in the air. It was so funny that we all laughed along with him. His wife Audrey said that she had never known him laugh so much. Apparently in the years that followed he never suffered from depression again.

Around that time I was invited to preach at Birches Green Evangelical Church in Birmingham where I had been on many occasions before. It is a small church that has known better days and the folk there are definitely in need of encouragement. I therefore rang the pastor, John Usher to ask if I could bring my house group and another couple along to share with the church what God had been doing in their lives. Pastor John agreed enthusiastically and after a couple of hymns I testified as to some of the unusual events we had been experiencing since listening to the Ellie Mumford tape. Different ones told their story, especially John and of his release from depression. After all of the talking we said we would like to pray for anyone in the church who wanted to be refreshed and encouraged. We started with the Pastor and his wife and they both received a clear touch of joy from God as they lay on the floor soaking in God's presence. Now I knew what the Lord was talking about when I got soaked in the rain coming home from work that day. All in all everyone in that church got prayed for that night, receiving a touch from God, through people who normally would not have done that type of thing and most of them were you might say in their latter years. It was truly amazing.

Meanwhile, back at Solihull Christian Fellowship it was decided to invite Steve and Jeanne Wood up from their home in the South West to come and talk to the church one Saturday following their visit to Toronto. We wanted to know first-hand from people that we knew well, what was really going on in Toronto. Well this turned out to be another watershed moment. Steve, in particular, was clearly different. His words always carried conviction and clarity but this time they were mixed with a gentleness and compassion not previously evident. The tears flowed from Steve at different points as he shared out of weakness and then when Steve and Jeanne moved out to pray for people again the floor more resembled a war zone than a church, with bodies prostrate on the floor meeting with God. I promise you this was not your normal middle class English church, not any more anyway.

Sylvia was one of the folk most impacted by this move of God and she moved into an area of spiritual sensitivity the like of which she had not known before. She also experienced a lot of emotional healing from her past and God did it with sovereignty and gently in a most quiet and unassuming way, albeit with bucket-loads of tears. In view of the fact that so many people were being touched by this move of God, we decided as a leadership to start Sunday night meetings where people could come and meet God and be refreshed. Sunday night meetings had not been a regular part of the life of Solihull Christian

Fellowship since its inception in the early 1970's and so it was hard to get people out. We decided that no pressure should be brought on anyone to attend these Sunday night meetings. If God turned up then things would happen and people would get to hear about it. We started with about 12 people and as more and more people were touched by God the numbers increased. At its height we were getting around 60 folk attending those *Times of Refreshing* Sunday night meetings and a few people even attending from other churches after their Sunday services had finished.

Inevitably with something like this, however, there was criticism. Indeed the whole Toronto blessing phenomena has attracted masses of criticism. Many respected theologians have been divided on the issue of whether this move has been of God or of Satan. I have no doubt in my own mind that whilst there have undoubtedly been excesses in terms of some of the so-called manifestations of the Spirit, that primarily this has been a move orchestrated by God himself. Through this outpouring (remember my soaking?) God has come close to people in intimacy, with his kiss and with a fresh revelation of his Father heart.

As Elders of Solihull Christian Fellowship we received criticism from inside and outside the church for allowing such self-indulgent behaviour. These comments of course were given serious consideration and after much debate and prayer it was decided that the *Times of Refreshing* meeting on a Sunday night would undergo a change of emphasis and would become more of a traditional style prayer meeting where we would concentrate on praying for the needs of those outside the church. It sounded good and spiritual, but something in my heart was ill at ease with this change of direction. As I saw it, God was still working on people's lives and it was like turning the power off in the middle of surgery; people would be left to bleed to death.

This whole debate became very stressful for me and I was getting lots of headaches and feeling very nauseated. Eventually I went to see the Doctor who told me that my blood pressure was very high and that I needed to go on medication. The fact of the matter is that I did not have the courage of my convictions (without cracking up physically) to say to Alan, Dave and Pall on behalf of the church of which I was an Elder that I believed categorically that we should continue with the *Times of Refreshing*. With my continuing sense of stress, however, allied to my feeling of being out of step with my fellow Elders, there was no alternative as I saw it but for me to request that I withdraw from

Eldership and ultimately continue my pilgrimage elsewhere. It was a hard decision to come out of Eldership and an even harder to leave Solihull Christian Fellowship a second time. It was difficult from the point of view of leaving behind friends and also the sense of disappointment that they may feel in Sylvia and me going. However, as I said earlier in my story I had by this time discovered that wonderful verse in Psalm 84 'Blessed are those who have set their hearts on pilgrimage, whose trust is in the Lord'.

The Bible makes it clear that that which is not of faith is sin and sometimes you have to make painful decisions just to get back into a place of faith, rather than just going through the religious motions. Better to be a God pleaser than a people pleaser, though admittedly it's nice if you can do both.

During these difficult times our family was dealt another blow when my son Ian became seriously ill and was diagnosed with encephalitis at the age of 18. The weeks of hospitalisation in intensive care, rigorous tests, and emergency surgery that followed were some of our darkest days as we truly feared for our son's life and were told to prepare for the worst.

We received wonderful support from our friends at Solihull Christian Fellowship, at work and in churches around the country. Even on Radio WM, Michael Blood on his Sunday morning programme asked people to pray for Ian's full recovery. No wonder I shed a tear or two at Wembley Stadium when we sang *Abide With Me* at the FA Cup Final of 2000 and it was not because Aston Villa lost to Chelsea, I was just so pleased to be there with Ian to share in that momentous day.

Mercifully, through the love, support and prayers of family and our church, and by the grace of our amazing God, and the skills of the medical staff who cared for him, Ian made a full recovery, and this traumatic period served to remind us of how fallible and precious life truly is. Indeed, even Ian's surgeon said that his recovery was really quite spectacular. I have referred in this book a couple of times to the God of surprises, now to that add the God of the spectacular.

Sylvia's service and our next steps

Sylvia, after many years of being at home for the children and undertaking a variety of cleaning jobs, then accepted a job as a care assistant. After three or four sorties into a variety of caring type situations, she actually found a job that she loved at the Prince of Wales Nursing Home in Solihull Lodge.

After being very nervous about going back into regular employment following so many years, Sylvia took to this kind of work like a duck to water. She found it personally very rewarding and gained a reputation of being an excellent carer. Sylvia also loved working at that home because of the superb way it was run by the Matron, Anne Barry, a former nurse at Solihull Hospital.

Sylvia developed a particular rapport with folk who were dying and also in comforting relatives. More than once it was put to Sylvia that she would make a good nurse in a hospice situation and as there is a Marie Curie Hospice by the name of Warren Pearl quite near to where we live, Sylvia decided to ring up and request an application form. To her surprise within days of filling out the application form she received an invite to attend for interview. Sylvia was successful in the interview and she began working at Warren Pearl as an auxiliary nurse, or as the new name decrees, a health care assistant.

I am so proud of what Sylvia has achieved since she has been working at the hospice, as indeed I am in awe at the wonderful work that is carried out by so many of the nurses who undertake this kind of work. My wife has found considerable fulfilment and self-worth as she has cared for people in this way. On one occasion when she and other members of staff were caring for a man who was a fanatical Birmingham City supporter, Sylvia contacted the football club manager, Steve Bruce, to see if anything could be done for this fan that would give him and his family a massive morale boost. She was thinking of maybe a signed shirt or football. However, one day while Sylvia was working there was a phone call for her. She was convinced it was me as she picked up the receiver and said "Hello".

"Is that Sylvia?" the man asked.

"Yes" she said wondering who it was.

"Hi Sylvia, this is Paul Devlin and I am ringing from the Blues training ground. I have your letter to the manager and I would like to come and visit Warren Pearl this afternoon. Is that okay?"

Well as you can imagine Sylvia was thrilled and excited. The news that Paul Devlin (one of the more popular players) was coming to the hospice caused a real buzz about the place. When Paul arrived he was accompanied by another player, Curtis Woodhouse. They went in to see the gentleman concerned, who by this time was joined by his family. They presented him with a signed shirt, which he immediately put on. Photographs were taken of this happy scene and the terminally ill man declared that it was one of the happiest days of his life. The two players were a credit to themselves and to Birmingham City Football Club. Within 72 hours of their visit, the gentleman had passed away and he was cremated in the football shirt that he wore so proudly. The family were so grateful for this gesture that had meant so much.

I've no doubt that incredible acts of love and kindness take place all over the country every day of this nature that never gets reported. Footballers in particular get a bad press and much of it is justified. However, there are many, who in their own time, visit the sick, attend charitable functions and make it possible for some to enjoy the happiest day of their life. Sylvia often came home and wept with me over her patients and we had some precious times praying together for them. Down through the years Sylvia has supported me so much in my work and what might be termed as 'flights of fancy', but now it was my very great privilege to support her in this work of caring that I know touches the heart of Jesus in a very special way.

As far as churches were concerned at this point in our lives, there were two of them that in the Solihull area were still flying the flag for the Toronto Blessing. As far as we were concerned this was the biggest thing to hit the Christian Church, maybe in our lifetime, and we wanted very much to be part of it. For a time we went to Arden Church about four miles out of Solihull town centre in the village of Knowle. We were quite happy attending services there, without making any long term commitment. Then, as He often does, God took a hand.

I was invited by my friends Phil and Christine to visit their church in Middleton, Lancashire for a weekend to talk about what the Holy Spirit was doing in the UK Church as I understood it. As Sylvia and I thought about that weekend the more convinced we became that we should invite Steve and Jeanne Wood from Wells to accompany us and indeed take the lead part in the weekend as they had first-hand experience of what was going on in and out of Toronto. Well having cleared this with Phil and his fellow church leaders, we duly contacted Steve and Jeanne who responded enthusiastically to our invitation to join us for the weekend in Lancashire. Suffice here to say that we had a wonderful time and

God moved powerfully in people's lives. One major thing that came out of that time was that two local churches decided to reform as one body and so pool their resources. On the way home Steve told us that he was due to be preaching in Solihull the following week and he would like it if Sylvia and I would join him, so that we could be available to work as a team once again when it came to praying for people. We agreed readily.

The church Steve was preaching at was the other one in Solihull that was running with the Toronto Blessing and it was also where Richard and Audrey attended (who we had stayed with when we came back from Cornwall) along with quite a few others who had left Solihull Christian Fellowship with us all those years earlier. I think that is why we did not attend The King's Church first of all. It was on our doorstep so to speak, but I guess we just did not want to have to humble ourselves again and say "Will you take us back?"

So it was that we did accompany Steve and Jeanne on that Sunday morning at The King's Church, Solihull and quite a morning it was too. The praise and worship band consisted of some really skilled musicians and they made a great sound, led as they were by an Irish guy who had an ability to get everyone, from the youngest to the oldest fully involved. It created a wonderful sense of intimacy with God. Steve preached powerfully and at the end of the service most of the congregation of about 50 started coming forward for prayer. As we laid hands gently on people it was clear that God was touching lives. Some laughed, some shook and some cried and some did all three. These were special days because in nearly 30 years now as a Christian, since giving my life to God in Westminster Chapel, I had only rarely witnessed stuff like this, though I had read about it in many books of it happening in far off lands. Now it was happening in our back yard and it was thrilling.

It was a very painful thing for us to leave Solihull Christian Fellowship, apart from leaving great friends behind, it also left us open to criticism, which may or may not have been justified. It was difficult, but what we were experiencing now was what we had moved on for, and we desperately wanted to know God in a deeper and more intimate way. The Toronto experience had made this possible and we wanted to run with it for as long as we possibly could. We did not want to go back to doing church as we had always done it and known it. We therefore started attending and enjoying The King's Church. We discovered it was part of Newfrontiers International, a worldwide family of churches led by

Terry Virgo. Terry, an ex-London Bible College student, now a leading International speaker and author, saw the whole thing start off from a small church in West Sussex around 30 years ago and develop to where it is now, impacting on many nations.

At the time of our arrival, the King's Church had three Elders, Graham Pearce, Stuart Webb and Paul Crabtree. They seemed to complement each other really well. They had been to Toronto together, experienced the blessing first hand and they led the church in a very relaxed, laid back manner, simply allowing God to flow through them, or at least that is how it seemed to us. At that time three other families made the switch from Solihull Christian Fellowship to The King's Church for the same reason as us. On one of our earliest visits to the church, Paul, one of the Elders (with whom we were to become really close friends) simply told us to "Chill out and enjoy God". We did that for a short time and probably would have done for a bit longer had we not been put on the spot somewhat.

On one particular Sunday morning, a young couple named James and Suzanne were invited to the front of the church by Graham, one of our Elders. Graham then came across to Sylvia and me and asked us if we would go out to the front and pray for James and Suzanne. Suzanne in fact was one of the worship team and also a daughter of Elder, Paul and his wife Carole. Other than that we knew little about them and that is obviously why Graham asked us to pray for them. As we stood in front of James and Suzanne, quietly praying, I became aware that Sylvia was struggling with something. I said to Sylvia "Do you have something you want to say?"

"Yes", she said with stammering lips "but it seems crazy".

With that Sylvia said, with a great deal of nervousness "I feel the Lord is saying don't worry for it will all be done and dusted by September."

James and Suzanne looked at each other knowingly and then hugged us tightly as if we were close family friends. Little did we know then but we were about to become that very thing. Later in the day after a very nice Sunday roast, the telephone rang and it was Suzanne. She asked if we were free to go round to their house for tea as there was something they would like to tell us. By 5pm we were sitting at their dining table enjoying a selection of sandwiches, cakes and cups of tea. Eventually the conversation got around to what they wanted to say.

"That was amazing this morning wasn't it James?" said Suzanne

James nodded his agreement.

"You could not have known what we were thinking Sylvia" continued Suzanne.

It transpired that James and Suzanne had been feeling a little bored. Both were as far as they could go in their present jobs, James as a teacher and Suzanne lecturing in law at a Wolverhampton College, so they wanted to do something a bit different. Suzanne had seen a job advertised in the Cayman Islands for someone to lecture in law and it fitted her qualifications perfectly. The contract was for two years and the job would start later that year – in September, just as Sylvia had said. James would have to get a teaching job, but they had been praying about whether this course of action was right for them. They had been asking for guidance and then Sylvia, who did not even know them goes and says it will all be done and dusted by September. That seemed very much as if it was God's confirmation to them.

Sylvia of course was greatly encouraged by this as indeed we all were. They decided to proceed and James applied for a job and got one without any hassle at all. It was indeed, just as Sylvia had prophesied done and dusted by September. James and Suzanne had to talk this through with their respective parents, but within a few months they were nicely settled into their luxury apartment on the beautiful island of Grand Cayman. Now I invite you to read the following article which I wrote that will take you into the next part of my story.

Dreams can come true

As we stepped off the Boeing 777 and descended the steps on to the concrete runway it was immediately apparent that we were somewhere exotic. The hot gentle breeze upon the face and the fragrant smells that were in the air were an instant reminder, as if we needed one that this was to be no ordinary holiday. Could it really be that after struggling to raise the money for a week in Blackpool or Torquay with their four children for most of our married life, we were now embarking upon a week in the luxurious Cayman Islands for free? This was all courtesy of our good friends, and I will never forget that phone call;

"Good evening! Can I help you?"

"Hello John, this is Carole, how are you doing?"

"Fine thanks" I said cheerily.

Carole went on, "Have you and Sylvia booked a holiday this year?"

"Yes we have," I said, "we are going to Scotland for a week in July, it is something we have wanted to do for years."

"Oh I see, Carole said with a note of disappointment in her voice, before going on to say, "well would you like another holiday?"

"Yes of course - wouldn't we all?" I replied with a hint of laughter in my voice.

"No! I'm serious," said Carole, "Paul and I would like you and Sylvia to go to the Cayman Islands to visit Suzanne and James."

Carole went on to say that Suzanne and James had requested for us to go and visit them and as Paul and Carole had some air miles they wanted to treat us. They booked the flight and did everything for us. It was simply amazing. Having come to terms with the initial shock, told the news in the office and arranged annual leave, it was all systems go. Our knowledge of the Cayman Islands was negligible and so we took to reading travel books and watching a video about the place in order to find out all we could. There are three small islands which make up the Caymans, they are Little Cayman, Cayman Brack and the largest (which is still not very big) and is where we would be going called Grand Cayman, the capital of which is Georgetown. The Islands are situated in the Caribbean between Jamaica and Cuba. The Caymans are a British colony the currency is the dollar and there is a great deal of wealth. The climate is most definitely on the tropical side and the temperatures at the time we were there were around 90 degrees Fahrenheit with a fairly high humidity. It is true to say that I counted the days down like a little child waiting for Father Christmas. I was so excited.

The day finally arrived for setting off and we took a 4.30am coach to London Gatwick in order to catch the 11am flight to Grand Cayman. It was such a great adventure. Safely on board the plane for an 11 hour flight (surpassing our previous longest trip by some 7 hours) we were treated to a couple of lovely meals, a free bar service and some good movies. We did have a stop for people to get off at Nassau in the Bahamas and for refuelling and then on for just over an hour to land at Grand Cayman. Having collected our luggage Suzanne and James were there to greet us enthusiastically with hugs all round and then off by car for the 20 minute journey to their flat, which they are renting for the two years they are working out there. The car ride was a mixture of excited conversation catching up on news from home and eyes looking out of the window not wanting to miss any of the scenery, where palm trees were very much in evidence across the flat landscape.

Driving took place on the left-hand side of the road, though most of the vehicles were left-hand drive as they were imported from America. Our hosts lived in a complex called Flowers Apartments consisting of about 30 spacious and luxurious two bedroom flats which were served by an open air swimming pool that was to be quite a haven for us to escape from the blazing sun during the course of our holiday.

At the time of our visit The Cayman Islands were six hours behind our British Summer Time and so after a long trip we were not late out of bed that first night. The air conditioning in the flat was superb, as it was in all of the shops and places of work on the Island, so we had an excellent night's sleep. Suzanne and James went off to work early next morning to teach law and geography respectively whilst we showered, had breakfast and planned our day. I heard on Radio Cayman that temperatures were expected to be 87 degrees with cloudless skies for several days. Just the job I thought, now the fairy tale could really take shape.

We were told that within a 15 minute walk of the apartments was a tiny beach called Smith's Cove, so we headed for that. What we weren't prepared for was that within minutes we would be dripping with sweat. We walked down Webster Drive with its sprawling Dallas/Dynasty-like mansions either side of the road with their long sweeping drives up to the impressive entrances. The trees were tall, beautiful and fragrant, with colourful exotic birds, including parrots, nestling in the branches. Pausing to take photographs along the way we eventually arrived at the beach.

Weaving our way through the trees and down a short hill which became increasingly sandy we were suddenly confronted with a most breath-taking view of this small cove with its white sandy beach, a handful of people dotted about under the many palm trees and the beautiful Caribbean Sea stretching out calmly before us. The sun was beating down from a clear blue sky causing the sea to reflect a variety of magnificent colours. We paddled for ages in the warm water, sat around on the sand and took in the idyllic scene. Not for the last time we were to say "Can this really be happening to us?"

Later in the week we visited two more beaches which were much bigger but equally beautiful in their own ways. Rum Point was gorgeous and it was there we took to sun-bathing in a double hammock with the ever-present sound of reggae music playing gently in the background - very romantic! We followed this up with a visit to the most aptly named Seven Mile Beach which gave the impression of what it might be like to be on a desert island.

Of course no holiday is ever complete, especially for the ladies, without a shopping trip. One morning we went into Georgetown with its many banks and other financial institutions. We walked a little and sat a little because it was so excruciatingly hot. Often we would nip into the shops just to enjoy the refreshment of the air conditioning!

A surprise event took place also, which for me was like icing on the proverbial cake so to speak. James had been doing some voluntary work at a Christian radio station called *Heaven 97* and as a result I was invited to be the subject of an interview about my life and faith. Following the radio interview I received a phone call asking me if I would go and preach at a church the next evening. Well I did and it turned out to be an amazing experience. It was an all Jamaican Church and we were given a wonderful welcome. The music and singing was vibrant and I really enjoyed preaching there. After the service the men came up and shook my hand but the women came up and showered me with hugs and kisses. Sylvia was most gracious, especially as the Church gave us a very generous gift of $137 (approximately £100) as a token of their appreciation.

Before we knew it, it was time to put away the sun cream and leave our very own piece of paradise to head back home, so armed with a bag-load of goodies including souvenirs and presents for the grandchildren, we eventually arrived back in Solihull.

Next time something really good happens to you let me encourage you to spread it around as much as possible, so that there may be more people who like me would still believe in fairy tales. For Sylvia and me, our visit to Grand Cayman were a little bit of heaven on earth. Paul and Carole have become wonderful friends to us over the years, it is interesting how in our walk of faith, God has given us at least one or two couples that we could get really close to for mutual encouragement at every stage. I appreciate every individual and couple that God has put in our path and I am still in touch with nearly all of them either by email, letter or telephone. I regularly thank God for every person who has added something to my experience of life.

Accidents and Access To Work

While all this was going on things had been ticking along quite nicely at work, though it came as a bit of a shock when the office I was working in, near to Solihull town centre was closed down and most of the staff, including myself were relocated back into the centre of Birmingham. I was placed in a large typing pool on the third floor of a 12 storey building called City Centre House. I was one of only two typists who moved from Solihull to Birmingham and it was quite difficult going from a pool of six people to one of sixteen. Even more difficult than that however was the trip from my desk to the toilet. It was quite a long walk down a corridor, through several swing doors and down some steps. When in the vicinity of the gents I had to make sure I counted the right number of doors so as not to end up in the ladies, kitchen or even the mop room. I was well used to travelling into Birmingham over many years so the actual journey did not bother me, it was just a case of getting started earlier to catch the bus to the train station and then hopping on one of the regular trains into Brum. All went well for a couple of years and then came the accident.

The train was just pulling into Moor Street station. I was a little later going into work than usual due to the fact that I had attended a Doctor's appointment. As the train slowed down almost to a standstill I got up from my seat and made my way to the exit door along with a handful of other people. As the doors opened I followed a couple of people and stepped off the train, white stick in hand. What happened in the next second or two remains a painful memory to this day. I had probably become a bit blasé when it came to getting off trains, having done it successfully for so many years. That probably accounts for the reason why I did not put my stick down on to the platform first. I simply stepped off the train like everyone else, but in so doing my right foot missed the platform and went down into thin air, pulling me off balance out of the train and causing my left ankle to be trapped under the weight of my body.

185

Apart from the actual shock of what was happening to me, the pain of having my ankle trapped under the weight of my 14 stone frame was excruciating as I hung there half on and half off the platform. Fortunately a young man had the presence of mind to pull me clear of the train and carefully take off my left shoe, as I screamed out "It's my ankle, it's my ankle! The pain is unbearable".

In a very short space of time I heard the sound of the ambulance siren and I was soon on my way to the City Hospital. Although my left ankle had swollen up to about twice its normal size, x-rays confirmed no break, but there was some soft tissue and ligament damage, resulting in me having to have a couple of weeks off work until I could at least put a little weight on to the ankle again. In truth though several years have now elapsed since that accident I don't think my ankle has ever felt totally back to normal as it is frequently swelling up.

When I did arrive back at the office I was advised by my manager that she had been told of a scheme called *Access to Work*. This is a Government run scheme that enables disabled people to have a taxi take them to and from their place of work and the individual only has to pay what it would normally cost them on public transport. The rest is funded from the *Access to Work* scheme. I had in fact known about this scheme previously, but much to the astonishment of some of my colleagues, I had chosen to ignore it and travel to and from work by public transport. The reason being was that I enjoyed the experience of travelling and meeting interesting people to chat with on my various journeys. In addition to that I very much appreciate the flexible working hour's scheme that is operated at the office and I did not want to lose that by having to have set times for my taxi. In the interests of safety and job security however I was persuaded to give it a go. In so doing I have made some most unlikely friendships and allayed a few more fears along the way.

My initial contract under *Access to Work* was with a local taxi company, but it did not last more than a few weeks, partly because they were looking for bigger contracts and partly because they did not like how long they had to wait for their money. The taxi firm in question, not wishing to leave me up the proverbial creek without a paddle, put me on to a taxi driver, who occasionally did some work for them.

His name was Noor Hussain and he quickly agreed to take over the contract and be my regular driver. Hussain and I quickly became good friends, though I have to admit that I was a bit apprehensive at first, possibly due to ignorance.

Hussain, like me in his 50s, was a very religious man being a devout Muslim. There were times when he would ask me if I would mind if he pulled the car over to the side of the road so that he could pray for a few minutes. I would agree to this request, but still felt a little uncomfortable. Rather than sitting there passively, however, I decided that I would pray too. I therefore prayed in tongues to the God of Abraham, Isaac and Jacob, i.e. the God and Father of our Lord Jesus Christ. Picture it: here were two very sincere men praying to God in a taxi, but were they praying to the same God? I think not and I hope to explain why I think that a little later in the book when touching on another topic.

When Hussain picked me up from work in the evenings he would often tell me of a particular bargain he had bought that day. He would rarely purchase something at its face value, but would nearly always barter to get the price and one day he amused me highly with the story of how he bought a whole fish for a huge knock down price. He was as thrilled as a little boy in a chocolate factory and following that episode I named Hussain 'the bargain man'. We started our own little tradition in that on the way home each Friday just before I got to the taxi, I would pop into McDonalds and pick up two fillets of fish. Hussain would bring two cans of pop and we would have our own little party. One day Hussain said to me that he wanted to take on another contract and it would mean that he would pick me up 15 minutes earlier in the morning and it would take me 15 minutes longer to get home in the evening. This was a schools contract whereby a carer would escort a child to and from school. Well on the first day of this new contract, which started in the afternoon, I arrived at the taxi to be told by Hussain that the lady in the back was named Ann. I got into the front passenger seat only for this lady to say "Oh know I don't believe it, it's John Flanner".

I must have looked puzzled and so she said, "You do remember me don't you?"

"I know your voice" I said.

"I should hope you do, Sylvia used to look after my twin boys" she said with a growing sense of frustration at my inability to pick up on the name.

Anyway the penny did drop and I remembered it was a lady by the name of Ann Shirley, a lady who was once at Solihull Christian Fellowship when we were there first time around. For the whole of that school year then Ann joined us in our many discussions on a whole range of subjects as well as on our Friday night fillet of fish parties. Ann also took Hussain's daughter Amner, for some after school English lessons. From time to time Hussain would take a short break from taxi driving, or even go back to Pakistan (or to be more precise Kashmir) for an extended holiday. During those times I had other Asian drivers look after me and I have got to know Sarfraz, Abid and Zubair. The driver I have travelled with most, however is Mohammed Zamir. In fact now that Hussain is away on a more permanent basis Mohammed is my regular driver. He is a young man with a wife and three daughters. Recently Mohammed was a very proud father because his oldest daughter, Noshin, gained entry into King Edward's Girls School, one of Birmingham's leading schools. Mohammed and I have become firm friends and we help each other out wherever we can.

Although the Friday parties have now stopped we do treat each other occasionally, though I have to admit I think Mohammed is leading the way on the generosity stakes, because he often greets me from work with some freshly cooked samosas to try out.

Prior to *Access to Work* I cannot remember ever meeting any Muslims let alone having them as my friends. The guys I have come to know have all been delightful In their own way, but in Hussain and Mohammed I have found two men who are both kind and generous. The way they care for each other within their extended families is a real challenge to us in the West also. We have had many discussions about our differing religious beliefs, but in the end we respect each other. If I had been brought up in Pakistan I would in all probability believe as they do. I do make the point, however, that I do not believe in the Lord Jesus Christ as my personal saviour because I was brought up to do so, but because I came to an understanding at the age of 21 that Jesus died for my sins and he rose again from the dead to give me not only forgiveness, but also the free gift of eternal life.

Back to my family, my son Ian and I not only share a love of sport, but also enjoy similar music tastes. Among the artists we share a common enjoyment of are The Bee Gees and John Denver. In the case of The Bee Gees, we went together to Wembley Stadium to see The Bee Gees in concert on their 30[thh] anniversary tour. It was to celebrate Ian's 20th birthday and we had a magical day together singing along to many of the great tunes composed by the Gibb brothers over the years.

As darkness fell over the old stadium it was an atmosphere I will never forget as over 50,000 adoring fans fully extended their vocal chords on numbers like *Stayin' Alive* and *Night Fever*. For sheer spine-tingling excitement it rivalled any football match we have ever been to. John Denver, the legendary American singer-songwriter is as I say another one of Ian's favourite performers. One of his big hit songs is called *Some Days are Diamonds*. The chorus goes:

Some days are diamonds/Some days are stone

Sometimes the hard times won't leave me alone

I think years can be like that to. Some years are wonderful and like diamonds, whereas by comparison some years are like stone. The year 2003 was like that for us, on 1st January Ian rang from the beautiful Trout Inn, situated in the heart of the Oxfordshire countryside, where he was working as relief manager alongside his wife of six months Clare.

"Hi Dad, it's Ian here, I just rang to wish you and Mum a happy new year"

Though the greeting was meant to be a cheerful one, there was nevertheless a sombre tone in Ian's voice and I responded with "Thanks Ian, but how are you and Clare?"

Ian hesitated for a moment before saying "We have a bit of a problem...Clare's walked out on me and gone back home to her parents".

I was stunned by this news, having no idea that there was any problem in their relationship. They had enjoyed a wonderful wedding day some six months earlier and both families were so proud as we celebrated a wonderful occasion. Clare had gladly given up a career in office work to join Ian and be trained together in pub management. Now, however, it appeared that the long hours of working together professionally and then slumping into bed exhausted in the early hours had taken its toll on their fledgling marriage. There was to be no reconciliation. Clare, who we had a lot of time for, is now with someone else and has a baby son, whilst Ian too is now in a happy relationship with Michelle, a former school friend, though he is now out of the pub trade as he does not want it to contribute towards another relationship break up.

A few weeks in this year of stone, it was time for Leber's Optic Atrophy to strike again in our family. My sister Joan, herself not in the best of health and divorced from her husband Neil, had to come to terms with a crushing blow.

189

Her oldest son, Matthew then aged 18 awoke one morning to find that he could not see very well out of one eye. A hospital appointment was quickly arranged and the same old scenario was about to be replayed. First the one eye deteriorated followed by the other a month or two later until almost all of the sight is gone. A series of vitamin injections slowed down the deterioration and possibly prevented a complete loss of sight, but all in all the loss was dramatic and devastating for the entire family, especially for Matthew and Joan of course.

I guess only a mother can know what kind of pain they go through, when it comes to seeing one of the children they have brought into the world suffer in anyway at all. Matthew is now 21 years of age and has recently gained a place at Birmingham University studying Philosophy, of all things, so we are all very proud of him. Joan also has a younger son, Andrew who is now 20 and living and working in Liverpool with his Portuguese girlfriend Monica. They met through online dating and that's not the only Internet romance in our family as you are shortly to discover.

More tragedy was to hit us the following month. My brother Paul had been idyllically married to Sue for nearly 20 years. Even though Paul had been registered blind since the age of 17 he still held down a job in a factory for over 25 years until taking redundancy a few years ago. Sue meanwhile had originally worked as a laboratory assistant in a school. Unfortunately she had an accident one day when a bottle of sulphuric acid fell out of a cupboard and all down her. It left her physically and emotionally scarred. The trauma seemed to bring on arthritis and slowly but surely over the years the arthritis spread further and further around her body.

Sue was never one to complain however, she had a wonderful sense of humour and she and Paul enjoyed some wonderful trips out on their narrow boat around the canals of the West Midlands and further afield, always accompanied by their pet dogs Sam and Lady. Sue underwent numerous operations and also injections of various drugs to try and reduce swelling and pain in her joints. She took it all in good part and when it became too difficult for her to go on boating holidays, they sold the boat and bought a luxury caravan in Weston-Super-Mare, where they enjoyed some memorable times together. In the March, however, of our year of stone, Sue developed breathing problems, was admitted to hospital, where she subsequently died after a brave fight. Sue was 42 years of age and she and Paul never had a cross word in all their years of marriage. They were devoted to each other and as a family we were all crushed by this loss, but this was nothing to what Paul must have felt. Many months later while Paul was still grieving he began to search for consolation in the Internet and corresponding with others who had undergone similar bereavements. He corresponded with several ladies who had experienced the loss of a beloved husband and one lady in particular grabbed his attention. Amazingly the lady concerned was also named Sue and her late husband was called Paul. After email correspondence and then lengthy phone calls they eventually met and a year or so later they were married. Paul and Sue have now sold their respective homes and bought a new one together in Reading where we trust they will both live happily ever after in the way of all good fairy tales.

In the midst of all of this grief and sadness came a phone call in the early hours from our daughter Allison still living in St Agnes, Cornwall. If you are anything like us, there is always a sense of alarm when the phone rings after midnight and on this occasion our concerns were well founded. Allison's trembling voice gave it away immediately as Sylvia bumbled in the dark to pick up the receiver.

"I'm really sorry Mum to have to call you at this time, but Sara has been badly beaten up by Steve".

At that time Sara was living just a short distance from Allison and her boyfriend Steve, an ex-Corporal in the Army was known to have a temper and a particularly jealous and possessive side to his nature. It turned out that Sara had received kicks in the face and to other parts of her body, sustaining in the process several broken teeth and many bruises, both physical and emotional. Though the physical bruises have healed, I would suggest that the emotional scars are still there today.

As happens in so many cases, Sara did receive Steve back, accepting his tears as an apology, but again history repeated itself further down the line and ultimately Sara had to flee from Steve while he was out at work one day. There is of course a lot more I could say about this, but all I wish to do is to highlight what was happening to Sylvia and me and how we dealt with it. I am a great believer in forgiveness, I preach it all the time, believing it to be the most wonderful word in the dictionary. One of the worst things I can hear in life is when someone says "I will never forgive them".

191

From a purely selfish point of view I believe that I need to forgive anyone who offends me for the sake of my own health. Unforgiveness eats away on the inside like a cancer, causing bitterness of spirit, leading to misery and depression. Finding the grace to forgive leads to freedom, health and joy on the inside. I have come to realise that unforgiving does more harm to me than it does to the person who has offended me. I also need to forgive others because in the Lord's Prayer it says "Forgive us our sins as we forgive those who sin against us". It is an awesome thought that if I don't forgive others for what they have done to me then God cannot forgive me for the many times I have offended him. In addition Jesus himself upon the Cross cried out "Father forgive them for they know not what they do". Jesus is my example and now as a Christian He lives on the inside of me and works out His purposes through me, giving me the grace to forgive. Having said that to forgive Steve for what he did to Sara was definitely one of the hardest things I have had to do. I will say this for my kids that they have all found the ability to forgive and for that I am very grateful, because it is a truly beautiful quality.

During this, our year of stone, if we take the John Denver song illustration, I did a lot of reflective thinking. Inevitably the whole issue of life and death came under my contemplative microscope. I seriously questioned my Christian faith as to just how relevant it was to me and the folk around me in light of all this suffering. I remember on the morning that Sue, my sister in law died, I was just sitting in an armchair feeling perplexed and angry. I wanted to play some music but nothing particular came to mind. I walked across to my CD cabinet, pulled out a disc from the top shelf (what I usually call a lucky dip, it has to be when you can't see) I put it on the deck and it was only when it began to play that I discovered it was Boyzone. I rejected the first three tracks, but as soon as track four began I knew this was the one. I put it on to repeat and sat down to listen. It was the song *No Matter What* and as I listened a fresh surge of defiant faith filled my heart and these words came to my mind:

No matter what they tell me / No matter what they do

No matter how tough life gets / I'll keep on loving you.

My world and that of others was being shaken, but I needed to make a quality decision that no matter what I was going to go on trusting in and loving God with all my heart. This whole issue of mortality came sharply into focus for me once again when the shock news came through of the sudden death of Maurice

Gibb, founder member of my beloved Bee Gees. I began to feel a deep sense of sadness over people who die without knowing God, yet they have given so much pleasure in their lives to so many people. I wanted all good people to go to Heaven and live for ever and my emotions were being bombarded with questions. I thought about the many decent people who don't believe in God and have Humanist funerals. I admire their honesty and lack of hypocrisy. I have often been puzzled as to why it was that people who had no time for God in this life then went through a religious funeral. Perhaps it is as some say, that all people who have tried to live a good life go to Heaven anyway. Is there a Heaven and is there a Hell? Does it really matter, when all is said and done we have no say in where we go, or do we? What about my Muslim taxi drivers, where will they go when they die? Is their religion the right one, or are there several right ones? Is it as, some say, that all paths lead to God?

In these days we live in a heightened awareness of terrorism. We see the effects of it day in and day out on our television screens. The human race, however, faces one common terrorist from which none of us can escape. The name of this terrorist is Death. The thought of death and dying strikes terror into the hearts of millions of people world-wide. The subject of death is something that is avoided by most people today. I once asked my son in law Phil what his thoughts were about death and he said that he was too busy struggling to live to think about death and it was a subject that he and Beverley never discussed.

Arising out of my months of thinking about this subject I put together a talk which I presented at a few churches called *'Putting Death Back on Life's Agenda'*. I think it was quite well received with many people, even Christians, coming forward for prayer as the thought of death held them in fear. I truly believe that death is something the human race needs to start talking about once again. Instead of different religions fighting each other over issues that separate them, they should along with everyone else, start loving each other and genuinely seek answers for the important questions. One thing is certain and that is when we die the truth will be known. It will either be the end and we will have fallen asleep for the last time, or we will discover that there is a God after all. We will either then all be in Heaven (if that is what it is called) or some will be in Heaven and others will be in Hell. Every person needs to face the issue for themselves and find some answers. Along the way if we find some things that help us to clarify the mystery of how to face our common terrorist, Death, then surely we should out of genuine love pass on what we have learned. My take on this is as follows:

1. I do believe in God as creator of all things. When I look at the vastness, intricacies and beauty of creation I find it easier to believe that a magnificent, loving person is behind it all that to believe that a whole series of explosions in the atmosphere led us to where we are today.

2. I believe that this God is pure and holy and that He set many laws into motion, one of which is that there is no redemption without the shedding of innocent blood. God hates sin, He cannot look upon it, and so has to do something about it. Because all of mankind was full of sin God took action. He decided that He would out of his own genius, make Himself totally vulnerable by coming to Planet Earth, as a seed and in a way known only to Him (our God) He planted himself deep inside the womb of a young woman by the name of Mary.

3. Jesus (God himself) was born of a virgin, therefore totally without sin, He grew up in a normal family and submitted himself to His parents for 30 years. He then went out teaching and preaching the Kingdom of God. He also healed the sick, raise the dead, did many mighty miracles and taught His followers to do the same by using their faith.

4. Jesus made many claims about Himself, including several mutually exclusive ones such as I am the light of the world, I am the resurrection and the life, I am the door to eternal life, I am the way the truth and the life, no one can come to God the Father except through me. I therefore agree with C S Lewis who said you cannot therefore label Jesus simply as a good man. He was either mad, bad, or who He said He was. If He lied then He has misled millions and tricked them into following Him, or if He spoke the truth then He is who He said He was, i.e. none other than God Himself.

5. Religious leaders were incensed by Jesus' claims and the Roman authorities were upset with Him because He caused riots by His so called blasphemous teaching and so Jesus was arrested and crucified on trumped up charges. God knew this would happen and it was all in

his plan to shed His totally innocent blood for the sins of the entire human race.

6. Jesus was then raised from the dead on the third day and He spent 40 days with His disciples. The disciples who had been hiding in fear were totally transformed by the resurrection of Jesus and after they were filled with the power of the Holy Spirit, they went out with incredible boldness proclaiming the message that Jesus was alive and they did extraordinary miracles in His name.

7. Jesus went back to Heaven and sat at the right-hand side of God the Father where He has all authority. God the Holy Spirit was sent into the world to fill believers with power to live for God and demonstrate His love in the world.

8. God's own sinless blood therefore has been shed for the remission of all sin. So will everyone be saved and go to heaven? I think not. In many places the Bible (which I believe is God's Holy word) states clearly that only those who believe in and put their trust in Jesus Christ as their Lord and Saviour will be accepted into Heaven. Some classic verses which helped convince me are:

"For God so love the world that he freely gave his one and only son, so that whoever believes in him will not die, but will have everlasting life"
John 3:16

"All have sinned and come short of God's standard. The wages of sin is death, but the free gift of God is eternal life". Romans 3:23 and 6:23

"Whoever calls on the name of the Lord will be saved" Romans 10:13

"God is not willing that any should perish, but that all should come to repentance and eternal life." 2 Peter 3:9

9. God is passionate about all of His creation; He loves every single one of us. People often remark that a loving God would not send people to Hell to burn in the lake of fire and that is true. The lake of fire is made for Satan and all his demons but clearly there are millions of people who will reject God's love and will end up in that place of eternal torment. It is absolutely vital that we consider the Gospel (good news) here and now and make an informed decision as to whether we are going to put our trust in Jesus Christ or not.

Look at it this way, if you wanted desperately to attend a particular concert then you would have to decide well in advance to get your ticket. It would be no good trying to gain entry on the night without a ticket. You may love the artist in question, but without a ticket you are not going to gain entry.

Whilst that is not a perfect analogy, it does highlight the point. If you want eternal life, to live forever in paradise with God where there are no tears, no sickness or disease, no war but love, peace and joy in abundance, where even the streets are paved with gold and you get your very own mansion then you need to decide here and now, while you are still alive to put your trust completely in Jesus Christ to apply His blood to your sin-stained life. This will enable you to stand before Almighty God on the great day of judgement in confidence that He will let you in because your sins have been washed away by His own perfect blood. It will have nothing at all to do with how good or how bad you have been, but it will have everything to do with Jesus and the fact that He has paid the price for your total salvation. Phew! No wonder I love Him!

That then is my position, it seems like a reasonable faith to have and the story has stood up to historical scrutiny. The power of its message has changed millions of lives down through the centuries from all walks of life. Ever since I first opened up my heart to Jesus all those years ago at Westminster Chapel I have never seriously doubted His presence with me. I don't always know His perfect will for my life and I still have many questions, but I have felt His closeness and known His touch so many times that I am convinced that if I should drop down dead today, I would wake up safe in His presence.

I do not know of any other religious leader down through history who has dealt with the question of sin (mine and yours) and the issue of eternal life in the way that Jesus has. Do you? My dear Muslim friends do not believe that Jesus even died on the cross for our sins, but are of the opinion that Judas Iscariot took the place of Jesus. If that were the case, who has paid the price for my sin and what about God's eternal law, "Without the shedding of innocent blood there is no remission of sin". Also if Jesus did not die and rise again from the dead, how come all of those Apostles were transformed from fear-filled individuals to being people of great boldness and power, many were martyred because of what they preached and the fact that they refused to deny the resurrection.

If I am ultimately proved wrong then so be it. I am certainly having a great time being deceived in that case. I would urge everyone who is reading this book to take time out to think very seriously about the terrorist called death and start searching for some answers. Another verse from the Bible says, "If you seek me you will surely find me, when you seek me with all of your heart". Please do not make the grave mistake (pun intended) of leaving it until it is too late. Your research just may lead you to a different conclusion to the one I have come to, but at least you will have given the most important question you will ever face, some quality consideration.

Achievements and awards

At the point of starting to write this book, my Dad was taken ill and subsequently suffered a burst duodenal ulcer. Along with other members of the family I was called to Dad's bedside at Good Hope Hospital in Sutton Coldfield as we were told it was unlikely he would live through the night, following an operation during which his heart actually stopped beating. Incredibly, Dad pulled through, but during his rehabilitation period he had a fall and broke a hip necessitating a further operation and period in hospital. Dad was later diagnosed with dementia and is now resident in a care home not too far from us in Solihull. He now has practically no short term memory at all and even his long term memory is now starting to fade. Having said that his general health is better than it has been for many years and thankfully for most of the time he is cheerful of spirit and a joy to his carers, especially when he bursts into singing some of those old music hall and pub favourites that he used to play on the piano.

I have undergone bouts of poor health and there have been further domestic traumas with some of our children, however on a brighter note, things have continued to go well at work and after 23 years as an audio typist I am now settling into life working as part of the Open Case Clearance Team at HMRC. I was not best pleased when I was first told that I was being transferred from the typing team to the open case team. For me this change felt uncomfortable and unnecessary, but like so many people these days, I wasn't exactly given a choice, and as with lots of changes in life it has turned out to be for the better.

Firstly, I am on a team with some really friendly people, even one or two men on this team, which is unusual for me, after all you don't come across too many male typists do you? Secondly it excites me to think that I am part of a team of about 20 visually impaired people working around the country for HMRC who are being trained on this open case tax work. Thanks in particular to a guy by the name of Dave Yates, who has become an expert in understanding how Job Access With Speech (JAWS) works and has therefore been able to write a multitude of helpful scripts to enable JAWS users to navigate around various screens, thus making it possible for the visually impaired person to be able to cut and paste information solely by the use of the keyboard. One of the other trainers, Penny Hilton, has just been awarded an MBE for the work she has done in this ground-breaking work. Although I have mentioned Dave and Penny by name, they are just two of the dozen or so people who have brought their skills into this very specialised arena and through their tremendous dedication have created job opportunities for blind people, that just a few short years ago would have seemed unthinkable. If it were up to me I would give them all a Knighthood, except the ladies of course, who would become the Dames in my story.

During the early days of my training one experienced tax officer said to me, "I don't mean to be disrespectful but you are never going to be able to do this job without sight, the screens are too complicated".

My reply, with a smile on my face, was to say, "My aim is to be able to do your job with my eyes closed!"

A couple of months later when I issued my first form to an employer without any assistance whatsoever I felt so proud, I was smiling from ear to ear, especially when someone collected the form from the printer and said it was absolutely perfect. I was heard to say, "I feel like I have just scored the winning goal in an FA Cup Final".

With that my aforementioned disbelieving colleague spoke up to say, "You've done it then! You can now do my job with your eyes closed".

I think HMRC deserves a huge pat on the back. There is probably not another Government Department or indeed any other business in the United Kingdom that is doing so much to create and encourage new working practices for those with a visual impairment. I have not been paid to say that either, not yet anyway!! When starting work on this team one of the people I quickly got to know what Heather Jacob. Heather, I soon discovered, is a committed Christian. She is part of a worship band by the name of *Vision* who are all part of Coton Green Church in Tamworth, Staffordshire. Heather told me that she and the other members of the band went into Swinfen Hall Prison in Lichfield once a month to lead the Sunday morning service in the chapel. Heather clearly loved those times and said how the young men, offenders between the ages of 18 and 25, really entered into the worship. I had not been involved in prison work for over 25 years but I said to Heather how much I would love to start again.

A little while later, after Heather had put in a word for me, I was able to go into Swinfen Hall and share something of my story with the men as part of the morning service. When I led them in a prayer afterwards it was such a joy when two young men came to see me to say that they had prayed along with me to commit their lives to Jesus. I went to the prison again a few weeks later and again it was such a joy to be able to share the good news about Jesus and then witness two more men giving their lives over to God. There is no joy in life quite like that, but the icing on the cake for me is to be able to sit and listen to the *Vision* band as they play their selection of traditional hymns and modern Gospel songs with a very definite Celtic feel to their sound. I am now a regular member of the team who have the privilege of going into Swinfen Hall prison to share my message of hope with the men and I regard it as such an awesome privilege to do so.

Now I am coming up to 60 years of age and in this year I am hoping to re-fire into a whole new orbit and getting this book published will be just a small part of that. I am still convinced that God's word to launch out into the deep is ongoing and will be until the day I die. I am deeply grateful to John Dolan, the Area Director, who first expressed appreciation of my writing that article and then for encouraging me to go on *Breakthrough*.

I am grateful to Linbert Spencer for writing the *Breakthrough* programme and for putting it together in the way that he did. It truly has been the most powerful personal development programme I have ever undertaken and it has most definitely helped transform my life. I truly believe that if the lessons in *Breakthrough* could be taught in our senior schools then many young people would discover their destiny, rather than wandering aimlessly through life and getting caught up in the binge drinking and drugs culture.

I am also grateful to the many people who have encouraged me over the past couple of years inside and outside of the office and in particular to all of those folk who have emailed me following my diversity awareness presentations saying that I have been an inspiration and that I should write a book. You have all played your part in bringing this to fruition as indeed have the many people I have written about in these pages. There are too many heroes to mention by name but suffice to say that I love and appreciate you all.

Now even as I draw this part of my story to a conclusion, God has had one more massive surprise up his sleeve for me.

The year 2006 saw the first ever Civil Service Diversity and Equality Awards. Imagine my surprise therefore when I receive a letter saying that I had been nominated for an Outstanding Achievement award and had reached the finals, to be held in London at Lancaster House. Several people had put forward my name as a nomination, but the one that really carried weight was from a man by the name of Nick John, with whom I have become really good friends. Years ago now I used to undertake audio typing work for Nick when he was a leading Tax Inspector in the Birmingham office and Nick also turned out to be on the same *Breakthrough* programme as myself, as one of the mentors. Nick had heard my *Fear, Fun and Faith* presentation on three occasions and he was keen to put my name forward for an award. Nick did a really thorough job and spent many hours putting his nomination together. I was so impressed with what he wrote about me, I would have chosen myself for an award! The great day came for the finals and Nick and I travelled down to London by train, enjoying some great conversation all the way. We duly arrived at the imposing and historic Lancaster House and after registration, sat down for pre-lunch drinks. Nick did a great job of describing the architectural style of the building together with many of the murals and paintings that decorated the walls. There was a real excitement about the place as people gathered from all over the country. After being called in to lunch we found our seats and continued our buzz of conversation.

Nick began a conversation with me spiritual issues and particularly around the issue of proof for the existence of God, the resurrection of Jesus etc. I said to Nick that I had seen a series of programmes broadcast on BBC 1 television a short while beforehand entitled the *Miracles of Jesus*. I said the series of four programmes on Sunday evenings had been absolutely brilliant, that I had learned so much from them and that I had encouraged friends to watch and write to the BBC in appreciation. The series astonished me all the more because it was written and presented by Rageh Omaar (known as the 'BBC's man in Baghdad' for his courage on the war in Iraq), who is a practising Muslim. I felt that to attempt such a programme was a very courageous thing to do on Rageh's part and I wrote to the BBC to tell them so and to offer my sincerest congratulations to Rageh. So there I was eulogising to Nick about the journalistic skills of the great Rageh Omaar, when suddenly Nick tapped me on the knee and said in a somewhat incredulous tone, "You are never going to believe this!"

"Believe what?" I said curiously.

"I think Rageh Omaar is standing right behind you," said a still disbelieving Nick.

"You're having me on!" I reacted in an equally disbelieving manner.

"Excuse me John", said Nick again, "but I am just going to creep around and have a look at his name badge".

I sat alone for a while as various other people chatted around the table and after a couple of minutes there was a tap on my shoulder before Nick said, "John I've got someone here who wants to meet you. Stand up and meet Rageh Omaar".

I shot to my feet, so excited and amazed that the very person I had been enthusing about to Nick had now turned up right behind me. I reached out and grabbed Rageh's hand as if he was a long lost son and squeezed it tight.

"Rageh I am so thrilled to meet you," I said in an excited fashion, "I was just talking to my friend about you and the series you did for the BBC, the Miracles of Jesus".

Rageh responded to me very warmly and said it was a very challenging programme for him to do and he described it as a defining moment in his life. We chatted together like old friends for quite a few minutes before Rageh was called away. I sat down feeling utterly gob-smacked and Nick too was amazed by the fact that the very person we had been talking about had suddenly appeared before our very eyes. It seemed like no time at all and we were into the awards ceremony. I listened most attentively to the citations for each award and marvelled at the contributions being made by so many people right across the Civil Service in celebrating the diverse nature of our workforce.

Eventually it came around to the category for which I had been nominated. The citations for the three finalists were read out and then the words "And the winner is...." were spoken by the Master of Ceremonies who was none other than Rageh Omaar of course. Then after what seemed like an eternity when my heart was beating fast, the words came out of Rageh's mouth "John Flanner".

In that moment I felt like I almost floated to the front of the stage to collect my award from Rageh, who tapped me on the shoulder and said "Well done mate, I'm really proud of you". I then shook hands with Sir Gus O'Donnell, Head of the British Civil Service and he presented me with a framed certificate and an engraved paperweight to celebrate my victory. I then had the privilege of posing for photographs and meeting with other leading Civil Servants, including Paul Gray, Acting Chairman of HMRC. Paul congratulated me and I said that I was surprised to find that I was the only person from HMRC to get into the finals as an individual. I asked Paul if this was indicative of a certain amount of apathy within HMRC towards Diversity and Equality issues. He said that was not the case at all because HMRC had more nominations than any other Civil Service department, 178 in all and the fact that I had been the only one, along with two other teams, to get into the finals, reflected so well on the diversity project that I had undertaken.

Nick and I travelled back to Birmingham on what had been a truly astonishing and exhilarating day out in the Capital. On the back of this award I have continued to travel the length and breadth of the country making my presentation, but now it has spread outside of HMRC. I have recently spoken to staff at the Cabinet Office for instance, taken part in a forum at the House of Commons and been interviewed on radio. It is all so exciting and now apart from this book I am launching my own business delivering motivational speaking to managers, teams and individuals nationwide about encouraging and equipping the next generation, *www.johnflanner.co.uk*.

Through my company I am aiming to offer my award winning *Fear, Fun and Faith* diversity presentation to staff in the wider business world, along with other talks that I have been working on. I now have a dedicated business website on which can be found all the details and I am also available as an entertaining and inspirational after dinner speaker. So you see there is no time to retire, because in re-firing there are so many people who are in need of the kind of encouragement and inspiration I am able to bring.

Final word

This book tells the story of my life up to the moment when I entrusted my existence to Jesus Christ, and the ongoing tale that has unfolded. Since inviting Him into my heart, I have still faced challenges and difficulties, yet I would wholeheartedly recommend and even urge you to consider making such a decision in your own life. Each individual has their own story, but I believe that God knows every detail of your life already and longs to be in a relationship with you if you will let Him in. If you feel that this might be something you are willing to do, then please pray this short prayer sincerely;

Heavenly Father, I recognise that you sent your son Jesus Christ into the world to make it possible for you and I to have a relationship through His death on the cross. We no longer have to be distanced from each other.

I recognise that I am a sinner and that I have previously alienated myself from you but the many wrong things I have thought, said and done.

I recognise that I have often known what the right thing to do is and have chosen not to do it.

I recognise that at other times I have done the right thing for the wrong motives.

Today I am sorry for the sin in my life and I turn my back on it, entrusting my life to you. Please enter in to my heart, as you promise to, and by your Spirit help me to live according to your good purposes.

In the name of Jesus

Amen.

Acknowledgments

Special thanks to Mum and Dad for so lovingly bringing me into this world to enable me to enjoy life as much as I do, to my brother Paul and sisters Joan and Susan for their encouragement.

Thanks to my children Beverley (and Phil), Sara, Allison and Ian for all their love and belief in their Dad, even when I have made it hard for them.

Most importantly of all, very many hugs and kisses to my beloved Sylvia, who has lived through most of this with me and without whose love I would not be what I am today. Thank you for your patience, darling!

Finally, to God be the glory, great things he has done and in the words of the great and delightfully named blind hymn writer of the 19th century, Fanny Crosby:

This is my story, this is my song

Praising my Saviour all the day long.

John Flanner

For more information on John Flanner please visit www.johnflanner.co.uk

Torch Trust

Torch Trust continue to provide a magnificent level of support to visually impaired people in the UK and around the world. Their Christian-based books and magazines are distributed in braille, large print and as audio books in ever increasing numbers. There is always a need for volunteers to learn how to transcribe their books into braille and to read them on to discs, and you can find out more about supporting this ministry by writing to them at:

Torch Trust for the Blind
Torch House,
Market Harborough
Leicestershire
LE16 9HL
Email: info@torchtrust.org
Website: www.torchtrust.org

Bitzaro to Buckingham

Acclaimed writer John Flanner is back with the second instalment of his autobiography that takes us from Bitzaro Palace on the Greek shores all the way back to Buckingham Palace on home soil. Starting with a series of traumatic events on holiday resulting in air ambulance ride back to England, John's story unfolds as he finds himself caring for his wife while facing new challenges in his working career.

The events on that fateful holiday and John's unswerving faith and fervour both personally and professionally, led to him receiving one of the highest accolades, an honour from Her Majesty the Queen. Displaying his heart and his humour in the pages, John's wonderful writing style captivates the reader who will likely experience and equal measure of laughter and tears as he takes them on a journey through the last ten years of his life.

Bitzaro to Buckingham details John's journey from retirement to refirement as he chronicles the launch of his full time career as a motivational speaker whilst caring for his beloved wife Sylvia. CEO's and stay at home mothers alike will relate to John's personable character as they read this inspirational story of how one man has defied the odds and continues to reach new heights as he follows God's path for his life.

***

Bitzaro to Buckingham is available in all good book stores

ISBN 978-0-9934175-2-8